LISTEN TO

YOUR MOTHER

LISTEN TO
YOUR MOTHER

What She Said Then,

What We're Saying Now

Edited by **ANN IMIG**

G. P. PUTNAM'S SONS
NEW YORK

PUTNAM

G. P. PUTNAM'S SONS
Publishers Since 1838
Published by the Penguin Group
Penguin Group (USA) LLC
375 Hudson Street
New York, New York 10014

USA · Canada · UK · Ireland · Australia
New Zealand · India · South Africa · China

penguin.com
A Penguin Random House Company

Library of Congress Cataloging-in-Publication Data
Listen to your mother : what she said then, what we're saying now / edited by Ann Imig.
P.   cm.
ISBN 978-0-399-16985-4
1. Motherhood—Literary collections.   2. Mothers—Literary collections.   3. Parenting—Literary
collections.   I. Imig, Ann, editor.
PN6071.M7L56   2015   2014040674
808.8'03520431—dc23

Printed in the United States of America
1   3   5   7   9   10   8   6   4   2

Book design by Gretchen Achilles

For my dear mom, Nancy Feingold

CONTENTS

FOREWORD

ANN IMIG

Founder and National Director, Listen to Your Mother

Listen to Your Mother: It's a cliché, it's the fifth command-
ment, and it's an imperative for curbing children young and
old from poor life choices like jaywalking and sixty-four-ounce
sodas. Because I am a mother myself, the word "listen" looms
largest in the phrase, and not only due to my constant attempts
to redirect my children's faces from a screen to my eyes, to hear
my words, *for the love of God.* I listen for and seek out the wisdom
in my mother's words. In the glorious moments when my mom
friends and I get a reprieve from patrolling our young, meting
out sustenance, and Tetrising our family schedules, we listen to
one another's truths, and to the experiences we share as women
navigating motherhood, daughterhood—and, well, peoplehood
in general.

Listening, in fact, makes for effective mothering—whether
we heed advice passed down from our grandmothers, obey a
parent, attend to a child, companion a loved one through a difficult time, or expand our experience of the world through the
simple act of hearing someone else's story. Listening forges

bonds between people, strengthens connections, and builds community.

Listen to Your Mother is also a spoken word phenomenon—a live-staged reading series born of women who write online and now sweeping the nation's stages, leaping from the Internet to podiums across the country in community celebrations. Listen to Your Mother gives motherhood a microphone, voicing the realities of mothers and mothering, of non-moms and caretakers, of sons and daughters—many of whom never considered themselves writers or performers—with stories so urgent they press from the hearts of people to the page and then to the LTYM stage, a small selection of which return again to the page, here in this book.

Geographically speaking, modern motherhood has become more isolating than ever, finding many parents without the benefit of extended family living under one roof or even in the same city. For some, the Internet likely feels as revolutionary as the first long-distance calls must have felt generations ago—connecting us with catharsis, commiseration, information, support, and, best of all, laughter, at any hour and from the comfort of our own homes.

Thanks to the Internet, however, now we need only Google parenting keywords like "special needs," "single parents," or "my four-year-old growls at anyone who says hello to him," and might find ourselves less alone by forming connections through reading blogs as varied in topic as the aisles in any bookstore. We create online peer-support networks, chat over virtual cocktails, and collaborate in online writing groups. Some of those connections bloom into confidants and friends. For some of us, writing through our days and nights, we not only make pen pals, we also find encouragement and inspiration, sometimes leading to professional connections and even careers.

My mothering coming-of-age coincided with the mom-blogging boom. My husband traveled constantly for work, and parenting a baby and preschooler alone through six-month-long Wisconsin winters (plus crib sheets, times stomach viruses) drove me to desperation. I took solace in squeezing humor from my sleep-deprived stay-at-home existence, and found comfort in writing through the chaos of a daily obstacle course that often started with a child poking me awake by my armpit stubble before 5:00 a.m., and by 5:00 p.m. found me laid prone on our Lego-strewn shag rug, allowing my darling sons to quite literally walk all over me. I shared my stories first with friends over e-mail, and then by staking out a little Internet carrel of my own—a blog that I named *Ann's Rants*.

For me, blogging reconnected me to an audience I didn't even realize I missed from my young-adult life as a stage actress. Instead of memorizing scripts, I found my own words to make sense of my experience of marriage and parenting in our overwhelming world. The richer my online life became, the more I wanted to bring all the creative vitality and peer support of the blogosphere to my real-life community, and release the literal voices from those online voices. I created LTYM to give voice to those words, and to make room for the voices of other mothers and men and women making sense of their worlds through writing. What started with one show at the Barrymore Theatre in Madison, Wisconsin, exploded into a national live storytelling series and social media phenomenon, and has now leaped to the pages of this book. Apparently, the voices of motherhood beg to be heard! As you read these essays about moms—from the executive to the stay-at-home dad, from the shtetl grandma to the rock and roll mama, from the Maya Angelou–texting matriarch to the reclusive wanderer to the grieving young widow, from hope to hilarity and heartbreak and back again—think about your own story. Consider writing it down. You don't need a blog, a book, or a show to find your motherhood voice—you need only listen.

MATRYOSHKA DOLLS

~~~~~~~~~~

MARY JO PEHL

M y niece was playing in the bathtub, having the time of her four-year-old life. Her parents were busy with the other kids as I was visiting one evening, so I volunteered to get her out of the tub and ready her for bed. She looked up at me from the tepid water. "Only my mom knows how to wrap me in the towel right," she coolly informed me.

She was right. I don't have children of my own so what do I know about wrapping a towel around a freshly bathed child? I am not part of the infinite *matryoshka* doll succession of humanity—someone's daughter giving way to another daughter giving way to another daughter, like Russian nesting dolls. I promised to do my best and bring her immediately to her mother so any mistakes could be corrected.

I'm not sure how it happened but my family has become overrun by these creatures, these offspring of my brothers and sisters. Each niece or nephew seems an alien of sorts, one we wanted and were excited about but we didn't realize we'd get *them* exactly. Like ordering mystery gifts from a Harriet Carter catalog: the ad declares, "For $5.95, we'll pick a special surprise gift for you!" and you get a package but you have no idea what it will be.

Me, I have known for some time that I cannot have children—if I want to sleep late. Of course, adoption is always a possibility but I could only seriously consider someone in their twenties or thirties. (Those kids are very hard to place, by the way.) And if they could live elsewhere and support themselves, why, I think that would work out best for everyone involved.

I find pregnancy and childbirth both spellbinding and a little, well, dreadful. I can't believe women even *walk* after giving birth. I'd insist on a wheelchair for at least ten years; in fact, I'd probably have to move into assisted living. Come to think of it, I'd probably need a service animal of some sort.

I have often interrogated my own mother about her five pregnancies and labors. She remembers each of them in great and vivid detail, and I listen like it's a horror story that has transfixed me, like she should have a flashlight under her face.

In a conversation we've had dozens of times, I tell her that were I ever to have children, I would be afraid of the pain. Every time she says, "Oh, but you forget about it right away." Every time she says, with a little exasperation, "And besides, Mary Jo, millions of women have done it for millions of years." And every single time I respond, "That doesn't make it right."

My mother had a heart attack a few years ago. A minor one as they go. Since then, she'd followed doctor's orders to the letter and was doing quite well. Then after one checkup, a nurse from the doctor's office called and left a message on her answering machine. It was the night before Thanksgiving, and in a chipper tone, the nurse informed her that the recent tests didn't look so good—but that she could discuss it with the doctor the following week. She signed off with a breezy "Now don't let this information ruin your holiday weekend."

It ruined our holiday weekend. One night as she sat reading, my mother put her book down and took a deep breath, trying fiercely not to cry. "I'm just not ready to say good-bye to the grandchildren," she said. And for the first time in my life I saw my mother as a woman. I mean, I've always *suspected*, I know I came from somewhere, but in that moment it hit me. She was human.

Because you don't always get that about your mother.

I realized I was once a baby in her arms. Her mother had given way to her, and she'd given way to me, laboring alone in a hospital room, as with all my siblings, in the days before fathers were allowed in the delivery room. Did she wonder what Harriet Carter surprise gift I was going to be for her?

The nurse's call was a false alarm that only required a minor change in medications. A few months later, I watched my mother with the latest baby. She has always been expert in the way she holds newborns, one hand cradling the head and the other forearm under the body so the baby faces her, almost nose to nose. She has a way of talking to infants with a low and caramelly voice. The tiny girl fixed on my mother, riveted, and flailed her scrawny limbs, never taking her eyes away from my mother's lovely face. My mother's gentle voodoo made for a lock between them, and at that moment, they were the only two people in the world.

It's been decades, but I realize only my mother knew how to wrap me in a towel right. After each bath, she'd comb out my hair, turning me around as I stood at her knees dutifully, and she'd fluff up my white blond hair with her long, elegant fingers. Every time she'd say, "It dries nicer this way." My niece knows her towel-wrapping mother for the artist she is.

WHAT MATTERS MOST

~~~~~~~~~~~~~~~~

ZACH WAHLS

Mother's Day has always been a big deal in my family's household. Or, as we like to call it, Mothers' Day. It's one of the notable differences of having two moms. During my work as an advocate for marriage equality, people will often ask what it's like having gay parents. The reality is that, just like most of you don't think about having straight parents, I don't get home for a weekend visit, walk in the door, and say, "Oh, look! My gay parents!" Just like you've probably never heard someone exclaim, "Oh, look! My straight mom and dad." After all, my moms don't live in a gay house, or drive gay cars, or gay park their gay cars, eat gay lunch, or have a gay dog—as far as we can tell. It's still a puppy, so I guess it's hard to say for sure.

But the point is that they aren't my gay moms. They're my moms. But they weren't always my moms—at one point, it was just my mom, Terry. In the late 1980s, she was a single lesbian physician living in rural Wisconsin who decided that she wanted to have children. This is not the setup to a sitcom or a punch line. A lot of people told her that she was crazy. But, between you and me, that was nothing new for Terry Wahls.

Now, most babies are conceived in a climactic moment of passion fueled by love and/or one too many tequila shots. But for those of us conceived using artificial insemination or in vitro fertilization, the process is much more clinical.

I was born in 1991, my little sister was born in 1994, and my mom Terry started dating our other mom, Jackie, in 1996. It was a whirlwind romance. They were married that same year. Or, well, not really married per se, but they had a commitment ceremony in a beautiful Wisconsin church, and invited friends and family to watch them exchange rings and vows. We all watched as they walked down the aisle to the theme song of *Star Trek: Voyager*—to boldly go where no man had gone before! Literally. I was a lot shorter then, so I was the ring bearer—the Frodo, as it were. Thirteen years later, I would be their best man when they officially tied the knot after Iowa became the sixth state in the union to recognize marriage between couples of the same gender.

At the time, though, the difference was lost on five-year-old me. Lots of differences were. Despite the normalcy—or boringness, depending on your point of view—of my family, I still got plenty of questions about having two moms. "Well, gosh, Zach, you didn't have a dad, who taught you about things like courage and strength and discipline?" Now, the guys who asked this question clearly don't know much about the women in their lives. I'm not even going to dignify that with a response. "Oh, well, okay, sure, fine, but who taught you how to shave?" No contest here. My moms didn't teach me how to shave.

I learned how to shave when I was in junior high. I was staying with my buddy Mike for a sleepover and in the morning his dad, Clif, noticed that I had a little peach fuzz on my lip. And he's this big hairy guy, you know, so he goes, "Hey, Zach, want to learn how to shave?" And I'm in the eighth grade, so I'm all like, "Dah, sure!" So he gets out a razor and some shaving cream and he shows me how to shave. Yeah, it was actually pretty anticlimactic. I'm not sure what I was expecting but it was not this moment where the music swelled, my shoulders broadened, my voice deepened, and I became a *man*. I cut myself, and I learned how to shave. It really wasn't so different from learning how to drive a stick shift—an important skill, but not all-defining.

"But, Zach, you didn't have a dad! Who were your male role models?" Just to be clear, after their commitment ceremony, my moms did not relocate us to some all-female compound in Lesbia-stan. There were plenty of great male role models in my life growing up: the aforementioned best friends' dads, male teachers in my public school, great mentors in my church, and, speaking as an Eagle Scout, incredible male role models in my Scouting units. There was no shortage of positive male role models in my life when I was a kid.

This isn't to *devalue* the importance of fatherhood, it's to highlight the importance of good parenting: At the end of the day, what matters most to kids is not the gender of your parents or the sexual orientation or even the number of parents that you have. What matters most to kids is whether or not you have a parent or parents who is or who are willing to put in the blood and sweat and toil and tears that it takes to sculpt little hellions into well-adjusted young adults. And if your parents have that—that love, that commitment, that dedication—if they have truly earned the title of "mother" or "father," the kids will be all right. I promise.

Now was it different having lesbian parents? Sure. Are lesbian women different from heterosexual women? In some ways, yes, and we do ourselves a disservice if we bother to pretend otherwise. Growing up, like any other kid would have been, I was well aware of the differences that existed between my family and others. And like any other family, mine was different from every other. My mom Terry was diagnosed with progressive multiple sclerosis when I was eight. We attended a Unitarian Universalist fellowship instead of a Christian church. My moms—both medical professionals and former athletes—put a large emphasis on healthy eating, physical exercise, and on not letting TV and video games rot my brain. Moms.

The fact that I had two moms and that they were both gay was certainly noticeable but in no way all-defining. This was due partly to my mom Terry's explanation of our family situation to me at a young age and due partly to the sheer normalcy—as far as I could tell—of everyday life. My moms still had to buy groceries and take me to swimming practice and balance their checkbooks, and unfortunately gay cars don't run on rainbows yet, so they still had to change the oil. Life with two moms, though certainly in some small ways different from the lives of those with a mom and a dad, was defined not by how others viewed us but how we interacted with and valued one another. We were defined not by some external perception, but by love, strength, and the commitment we made to one another to work through the difficult times so we could enjoy the good ones. That's what makes a family. And that's what matters most.

THE MEAT GRINDER

JEN RUBIN

My grandmother was a formidable woman and far from any stereotype of a doting grandmother. She grew up in a shtetl in the Ukraine in the early 1900s until her family fled the Cossacks when she was sixteen on a ship to Ellis Island. As a young teenager her job was to strap a sewing machine on her back, walk miles to town, sew for a gentile family during the week, and walk home for Sabbath. Family lore has it that it was on these walks that she developed her beautiful singing voice, trading songs with Russian peasants returning from the fields and Jewish and Gypsy travelers.

In New York City she was a well-regarded singer in the fairly obscure Yiddish folk-singing community. My grandmother leading our extended family in song during holidays was the best part of each holiday. But that didn't mean I wanted her in my living room, day in and day out, trying to get me to help her record her songs. Yacov, her boyfriend, spent a great deal of time at my house. He would put on his most dapper tweed, board a bus, and spend the day singing with my grandmother. They loved to record themselves and called me away from the television every few minutes to help them. They would sing a song and stop the tape. Rewind the tape. Listen to their voices and stop the tape. Rewind again. Then start the process over and re-record their voices. I knew they were messing with me. These were intelligent people that fled one continent and successfully made their way in another one. Tape recorders were fairly simple machines in the late 1970s. Rectangle boxes that could only play, record, fast-forward, rewind, and stop.

When I was a young teenager, my favorite way to spend a summer day was sprawled out on my parents' bed watching reruns of sitcoms. My grandmother kept pulling me away from the television because she wanted me to know these songs. She wanted me to hear the songs of the Jewish diaspora. She wanted me to know the music of my family. To her this was the music of home. I just wanted to watch *Laverne & Shirley* in peace.

Music wasn't the only lesson she offered that I ignored as a young teenager. My grandmother had an unshakable confidence in herself. It didn't hurt that she was beautiful. At least everyone told me how beautiful she was, though through my teenager eyes I had a hard time seeing it. But the facts stand on their own. At sixteen, on the ship from Russia to Ellis Island she won a beauty contest. She was often pulled off the factory floor where she worked as a seamstress in the garment district to model the clothing they were manufacturing. She looked that good in a skirt. Her self-possession went deeper than that. She had an unwavering belief in herself and didn't really understand a grand-daughter who did not share this trait. I was the kind of teenager who hid behind my hair and hoped not to be noticed. This approach didn't work well for me as a teenager and it wasn't working out so well in my young adulthood either. My grand-mother, concerned that left to my own devices I would never marry, intervened.

One holiday she pulled me aside to tell me that when I married I would inherit her meat grinder. I stared at her blankly, wondering how a meat grinder could overcome my inability to flirt. When I didn't say anything, she leaned in to me and said, "Let people know." At first I joked about this with my friends. Should I post an ad saying, "Quirky anxious twentysomething comes equipped for marriage with good cheekbones and a meat grinder"? But I couldn't get her phrase "Let people know" out of my head. I had made an art form out of not letting the men I loved know how I felt about them. I spent two months sharing a car and tent with a friend I was in love with and never managed to find the opportunity to mention it. I was in unrequited relationships. You might wonder how it is possible to be in an unrequited relationship. But trust me, it is. I did it twice. But no more. From now on I was going to "let people know." The following year, when I realized I was in love with my then boyfriend, I proposed.

The proposal was accepted. A wedding occurred. Two years later I was living in Madison, Wisconsin, and too pregnant to travel to New York for Passover. One night as I was falling asleep I realized it would be my first Passover without my grandmother leading the songs. I was surprised by how bad that made me feel. The next morning I called my mom and asked her to get a tape recorder and a cassette and sit with Grandma and help her record the songs and express mail it to me. So they did. During the Seder, every time we got to a song I turned on the tape recorder and let my grandmother lead us. Even at ninety and through the crackle of the cheap tape recorder, her voice sounded strong. I could picture her standing up and singing, *"Oyfin veg shtayt a boim"* (On the road stands a tree), and waving Yacov off if he started to harmonize during her solo. It sounded like home.

IT'S ALWAYS BAD NEWS

MARINKA

Let me just tell you this and save you the suspense. When you get a call from your kid's school, it's never good news.

It's never "We were just talking about how you are the best mom in the whole school and would you give tips to the other moms so that they could be more like you." Nor is it "Your child is just too smart. His teacher is requesting his immediate transfer to the PhD program."

It's always a "she threw up" or "he has a fever" or "both of your kids have lice—come get them the hell out of our school." That's why when I see the school's number pop up on my cell phone, I know I'm really in for something.

So I get a call from the school and the nurse tells me that my kid was hit with a ball in the eye and that he's in pain.

And I'm thinking, *Ball, eye, pain* but also, *I still have work.* So I ask to talk to my son and he says, *Yes, it hurts, and also stings, although the stinging may be the same as the hurting and it doesn't look like I'll be able to do homework tonight.*

I tell him that I'm busy and that this isn't a good time for an injury but that I'll try to reach his sister and she can pick him up in about an hour.

And he says AN HOUR? and I can sort of hear a gasp in the background and I say, Yes, an hour, maybe fifty-seven minutes, because what am I, some sort of a professional time estimator?

Then we hang up and I resume my game of solitaire. Seriously, why is that stuff so addictive? So stupid and yet so addictive! There's practically no strategy, but how fun is it when you win and those cards bounce around your screen? So rewarding!

Anyway, we hang up and then I think. Huh. Hit in the eye. Eyes are important. What if it's bad? Bad as in NOT GOOD? That would be bad. Wait, is this what mothers are supposed to do? Spring into action when their kids are hurt?

So I call back the school and say, "I'm on my way," and the woman on the phone says, "Oh, good, because usually the swelling goes down pretty quickly, but it's not in this case." And as soon as she says that, I think two things: 1. Why didn't she say so when she called? and 2. OMG, MY BABY!

I shoot myself out of a cannon to get to school, and the twenty minutes it takes me to get there is filled with images of my son's eye hanging on by a thread out of its socket (I'm not an ophthalmologist, so I'm not sure that's how eyes work) so I prepare myself for whatever gross shit may be waiting for me.

And then I get to school and I see him sitting there and I look at him and there's no little jar with his eye in it on his lap, so I am relieved, and then I look at him some more and turn to the nurse and ask, "Which eye is it?" because I can't tell. And she points to the right eye and says, "See the swelling?" and I look at it again and maybe, if I squint, and tilt my head to the side, I can see the swelling. But I really can't.

But I am so relieved and happy that my son is okay and I take him to the doctor just to have it checked out and she does all those doctory things and says that I should keep an eye on him to make sure he's not passing out or throwing up or speaking in tongues or joining the GOP and he should probably not do too much homework tonight and he sighs as though this is a big disappointment, but if that's what's medically necessary, he's prepared to follow doctor's orders, for health purposes only, of course.

So all's well that ends well. And that particular day ended with my feeling very, very relieved and my son feeling very, very like not doing his homework. But still, the whole incident just underscores my original point. Whenever the school calls, it's never good news. It's probably best to block the number.

I FELT LIKE SOMETHING

MEGAN STIELSTRA

Six weeks after my son was born, at that routine postpartum checkup, my doctor asked *how I felt*. This is a tricky question for someone who's recently had a baby; I mean, I can't speak for anyone but myself, but somewhere between the "How do" and the "you feel?" I exploded all over the poor woman: hormones, no sleep, indescribable love, indescribable fear, and where do you put it all? "That baby doesn't even *like* me," I told her—there was Kleenex and snot and breast milk all over the place, it was tragic. "And: I don't know what a *boppy* is! And they say to chart his poop so—is there, like, a spreadsheet? And then I've got these aunts who wanna bring me dinner, but then they ask about the baptism, and I don't believe in God or the Divine or *anything*, really, so is it okay to take their casseroles?"

"This is all totally normal," my doctor told me. She must've repeated it fifteen times. "Here's your paper robe—*totally normal.* Jump up on the table—*totally normal.*" Routine ultrasound to check on a minor cyst she saw during my pregnancy—*totally . . . oh.*

It's the single syllables that change everything. Your dentist says *oops*. Your pregnancy tests says *plus*. Your gynecologist says *oh*.

Later, after some tests, we sat on opposite sides of her desk and she explained that an ovary is the size of a cherry tomato. And a cell the size of a grain of rice had grown into a tumor the size of a tangerine. Which had then swallowed my ovary.

How do you react to news like that?

When I look down the line of my life, there are these moments—my parents splitting up, my first heartbreak, losing a job that I loved—and I cried or panicked or locked myself in a room playing Smiths albums on repeat, whatever: I felt *something*. But when that doctor told me I had a tumor? Nothing. Not sitting there in her office. Not later that night, telling my husband and holding our little boy. Not walking into emergency surgery the next morning—*nothing*—right up until I opened my eyes and my doctor told me she'd got it. Everything was suddenly fine. One day you're already dead, the next day you're back at the office and I cried and thanked her and drank my juice—after all of *that*, she said, "You're lucky you got pregnant. If it hadn't been for the ultrasound, we probably wouldn't have caught it in time."

In that moment, I knew exactly what I felt. I felt—*Something*.

It was so close. Do you know what I mean? Like when I'm on my dad's fishing boat in the Pacific, out there in the middle of nowhere, surrounded by blue, can't tell when the sky begins and the water ends. It is vast. It is still. It is—*Something*.

Or: For years, I lived in Humboldt Park, west at North and Kimball, and a few blocks from my apartment was this church. It was really small, not more than a storefront, but the singing that came out of that place was like nothing I'd ever heard. Every Sunday I'd get coffee at Dunkin' Donuts and sit on the curb outside that church. I never went in—there are a lot of things that happen inside of a church that I know are not for me—but sitting outside? I could have the parts that felt like—*Something*.

Or: My son is three years old now. He is awesome. He thinks he's Superman, which sounds very cute except we live on the third floor and he keeps trying to fly. Last week he stood at our balcony door in his red and blue costume, nose pressed to the glass, and said, "Mommy, let me out. I'll put my arms out far; I'll go high up in the sky," and of course, what I did then was check that lock, but what I realized is this: Our children save us. They illuminate what's been there all along. They make us better than we ever thought we could be. My son really is Superman. Without him, I'd have never had that ultrasound. Without him, the tangerine would have grown into a grapefruit. Without him, I might not be standing here today, and for that, I will believe. Call it God, if you like. Call it The Divine.

I call it a start.

A YEAR AT THE LAKE

~~~~~~~~~~

JENNY FIORE

The night before my husband deployed to Kuwait, I stood in our living room—vast, unpainted, still not feeling like home—and kept an ear open for our baby monitor. Our daughter, Elizabeth, then nineteen months old, was just starting to put together small sentences. I couldn't make them out over the scratch of the white-noise machine. Something about owl babies?

For many days, we'd been preparing her for this moment, for the fifteen months that lay ahead. "Daddy loves you," I heard my husband say. "I have to go bye-bye for a long time." There was no reply, only the rocking chair's creaking rhythm, going so much faster than usual.

My husband, Blaine, doesn't cry. He's a Green Beret. But when he comes to the bottom of the stairs, he looks deathly. "That was some sad shit," he exhales. His mouth is a squiggle. The lines around his eyes are curved a new way, like parentheses. We fall into each other's arms in a weird place in the hallway, not quite the hallway, not quite a room. We can't believe this is happening to us.

I save the rest of my tears until we're driving into the airport parking garage. Blaine holds my hand and, knowing there's nothing to say, says nothing. On the way home, I realize it's gotten cold out. It's dawn, and the streets are gray and empty. Oscar Mayer's drab, prisonlike packing plant towers over me at an intersection, and I think of what Blaine's quarters will be like. Like a jail cell. It's for him my heart is breaking. The year ahead stretches out before me like one of the Great Lakes. I know the other side is thataway, right over the horizon. I just can't see it.

It's not like we never talk. Blaine calls every three or four days. Elizabeth learns to do more than nod at the phone, but the transatlantic delays confuse her. Sometimes she hands the phone back to me just as Blaine's answering her, or worse, saying, "I miss you." The words fall into the air, sounding so small.

Blaine makes the sweetest video from his quarters, which do look like a prison. Behind him there's a gray locker and porcelain basin surrounded by Elizabeth's finger paintings and snapshots. "How about we sing some songs?" he says, tuning his electric guitar. "What song do you want to hear?" He waits, and she actually answers. "'Twinkle, Twinkle'?" he replies. "I like that song, too!" I've fed him data, told him the books and songs she loves. So we create for her the illusion of conversation. "How about we do some dancing?" he says. "YES!" she screams. "What song?" he asks. "'We Got the Beat'!" she screams. "'We Got the Beat'?" he says. "I like that one, too." He turns on a boom box and goes apeshit dancing to the Go-Go's. Hopping, twirling, leaping, doing the monkey—and Elizabeth is overjoyed. It's perfect, and I'm so grateful. Yet I'm mad it's all we can do.

While Blaine is gone, the following things happen: Elizabeth starts speaking in sentences. She learns to ride a trike, and then a bike with training wheels. Our friend is killed in Iraq. His wife tries to kill herself. Blaine's grandma develops dementia. Elizabeth grows six inches and moves out of her crib. She potty trains herself and regresses. She pees in the floor vents and draws on the walls. She learns the alphabet and how to count to twenty. We plant gladiolas and dahlias, which bloom and die. I don't even think about masturbating, not once. I keep having to regroup, to remember where it was this family was going. Treading water is hard.

At every turn, I feel Blaine's absence. There's a photograph of me in a party hat at Elizabeth's second birthday, singing with her on my lap. In it, I'm wondering where my camera is, wondering if anyone's getting this for Blaine. My sweater's a bright happy green like the color of a sports drink, making me look that much more weathered. Which I am. It's been four months, and already I'm run-down by having to memorialize it all for my husband. By having to do it all for our daughter. By that cold fucking lake that goes on forever in front of me. Every time the camera clicks or the camcorder beeps, I know we're not really living our life.

More than halfway into the deployment, Elizabeth and I are at a local gym for toddler playtime. She hates leaving, and I know it will end in a theatrical mess, but I go anyway. See, more than she does, I need the gym, the zoo, the petting farm. I need the pet store, the playground, the pool. I need these in order to keep my child happy enough, occupied enough to not break me.

But when open gym ends, it happens. Screaming and kicking, she clamps onto a fistful of my hair and pulls, and my stress and anger suddenly boil into a wrath so fierce it scares me. I'm harsh with her in front of strangers. I get in her face and shake my finger so close to her nose that I can feel her breathe. I growl that she will never come back to this gym. NEVER. During our drive home, I scream terrible things. She laughs. She sings. I feel like a freight train barreling out of control. I tell her to shut up. I fantasize about slapping her. I think I want to make her cry, to show me that she gets it, or maybe to make me stop what I'm doing?

At home, I send her to the bottom of the stairs, to the "naughty step," and I go into the bathroom to splash water on my face. I look old. I don't think I've brushed my teeth for days. I scrunch up my face to see how I look when furious, to see what my child just saw. Such a feeling of self-loathing comes over me that I want to punch the mirror. I think of my daughter's small body in my arms six weeks before Blaine deployed, of the way I cried when I nursed her that last time, not wanting to wean while her daddy was gone, not sure she could take that much loss at once. I knew then that I would always have to love her in a context beyond my control, in an imperfect world that deals us difficult choices that sometimes feel not like choices at all. But I had no idea it would be like this.

When I go to her, I know she's been crying. She's red-faced and snot-nosed and so much smaller than she'd seemed just a half hour earlier. I sit on the naughty step with her, where I belong, and tell her I'm sorry. I try to explain, but there's no way to explain. She's only two and a half. She needs to throw tantrums. It's her right to laugh when Mom gets mad. She's supposed to draw on the walls and forget how to use the potty. "I always love you," I tell her. "Even when you're naughty. Even when I'm naughty. I always love you."

We sit for a while, holding hands, and look out at that cold lake ahead of us, me knowing we are running out of stepping-stones, and her somehow still trusting me when I say the other side is out there. And that we're really almost to it.

THE BROKEN BOWL

〜〜〜〜〜〜

JENNIFER BALL

As far as bowls go, this one was nothing special.

It wasn't particularly beautiful, artistic, or unique in any sort of way.

When my husband and I moved into our first house, my mother-in-law came over one day with a large cardboard box. "Dad and I are moving into a condo," she announced, "and I thought you could use some of these things for your kitchen!"

We unpacked the box together, and as each item was pulled from its corrugated confines, my mother-in-law told me where it was from, and sometimes, a funny little story that involved said item.

There were clear glass bowls and salad plates and kitchen towels. A pitcher, a platter, and then she pulled out the bowl.

As I said before, this bowl isn't breathtaking. In fact, looking at it now, I'd say it's rather dated. It belongs in a kitchen heavily accented with hunter green and cranberry red. With some gingham-checked seat cushions and valences.

It's a pasta bowl. A very large pasta bowl. At the time, it was just my husband and me, and I remember thinking to myself,

"Yikes . . . what would I use that for?" Our meals back then were small, simple meals for two. Never a huge meal that would require a vessel such as the one before me.

After she left, I got busy washing and putting away my new things. The glass bowls were used immediately, for they were the perfect size to hold my nightly pregnant-lady portion of ice cream. The salad plates were ideal for our sandwiches and individual slices of whatever was chosen from the freezer for that evening's sup.

Then the four children arrived. One after another. As they grew bigger, so did our meals. As any mother knows, pasta is a childhood staple, and as my brood burgeoned, I found myself reaching for that giant pasta bowl with increased frequency. At least twice a week I placed it in the middle of the dinner table, the steaming mound of spaghetti or linguine or penne glistening with butter and slowly melting Parmesan cheese.

Too large for the dishwasher, this bowl was diligently washed after these meals, dried, and put away in its spot in the cupboard above the double oven. If I had to hazard a guess as to how many meals it served us during our marriage, I'd say well into the hundreds.

And then our family broke.

My husband left. He took nothing with him, only his golf clubs, his suits, and his car. His new life awaited him, you see, and I think taking reminders of the old one scared him. Intimidated either him or his new love.

So I was left with the children, the house, and everything else. Including the big bowl.

Our lives took many turns over the next few years. When my

ex-husband stopped paying child support, the turns became plunges into dark abysses, and we lost that house with the double ovens, the arched doorways, and the granite countertops.

Our new home, the rental I was able to get thanks to an angel disguised as a landlord, has a big kitchen. It's not fancy, but it'll do.

I've now become a master pasta maker; it's amazing how crafty one becomes when faced with near poverty. A few eggs and some flour become dinner, and a delicious one at that. Many nights we have sat at the table, our big pasta bowl filled with thick, hand-cut noodles.

We just had that dinner last night. The pasta bowl sat in the sink, waiting patiently to be washed and put away in its new spot.

In a hurry this morning, I saw the bowl and despite knowing better, I tried cramming it into the dishwasher. I stuck it in there, on its side, and almost immediately it fell over, hitting a plate.

I knew what had happened before I looked.

Our bowl was broken.

Our beautiful pasta bowl was broken, lying there in the dishwasher like a ceramic Humpty-Dumpty. I was surprised at the emotion that flooded over me as I picked out the tiny shards and the bigger pieces. And as I stood there in the kitchen, the dark autumn sky slowly lightening up outside, I tried to put it together again.

My son Henry walked in at that moment. "Oh no!" he said in his sleepy adolescent voice, "our bowl!" He tried, along with his mom, to put the pieces back in place. "Can't you glue it?" he asked me, with a look in his eyes that made me ache.

"I don't think so, Henry."

He pondered the broken bowl, and said, "But we've had this bowl forever. What are we going to use for spaghetti now?"

I shrugged. "I don't know," I said. "We'll have to find another one."

As each of the kids made their way into the kitchen after taking showers and getting dressed, their eyes settled on our broken bowl sitting on the counter. Their reactions were all eerily similar: a gasp, a statement, "Our bowl!" and then they'd touch it, try to put the pieces together.

I didn't have the heart to throw the pieces in the garbage before I left for work. I left it there, on the counter. And as I drove along the highway I thought about our bowl.

I thought about how we, as parents, break our backs and sometimes our checkbooks trying to ensure that our offspring will have good memories. How we try to make moments into something special, something amazing.

For parents who are in a similar boat to mine, those of us struggling financially, it sometimes feels as though we cannot possibly do or buy what it takes to create those memories. Those snippets of time we want our kids to look back on and smile.

I realized, this morning, that it doesn't take magic or money or even much imagination to create these feelings, these moments.

Sometimes all it takes is a hand-me-down bowl.

MO'BETTA MAMA

TASNEEM GRACE TEWOGBOLA

It was a Miss Sofia moment.

I was feeling bad, I was feeling migghhttyy low.

The day dragged long. The sun threatened to never set. The girls turned my name into a two-word song, stuck on repeat: Mommy, Ummi? Mommy? Ummi? Mommy? Ummi, Mommmmmy?

The baby tugged my skirt. I tripped and stepped on her hand.

The three-year-old unplugged the computer—yes, by accident but so what?!—while I was typing.

The six-year-old said she "forgot" to wear panties under her school uniform.

The eight-year-old told me she needed construction paper for a school project an hour or so *after* we got home.

All day a tribe of 18,000 red-bellied fire ants threaten my tribe with a steady, fearless march through the kitchen. Where the heck are they coming from?!

And then, after I slide bowls of dinner onto the table, my daughters ask, "Can I just have rice? Without the greens?

"And without the black-eyed peas?"

Who doesn't like my world-famous curry and coconut milk black-eyed peas?

What's wrong with these kids?

Then I check the time. Awww, hell naw!

Only 6:13 p.m.

Bedtime will never come.

With my husband rightfully in Tennessee helping his mother, I am holding down the fort, solo—so, so, so low.

Like I said, I was feeling down, not myself, sweaty and suppressing a scream.

"After every hardship comes ease," promises the Quran. But I was desperate, up to my earlobes in "hardship." I needed ease, right now.

So I called, actually texted, my mama. Four words: Overwhelmed. Alone. Outta Balance.

(Please note: I am the daughter of a dynamic, soul-filled, and Soul-Full woman. During my entire childhood my father called her "The Queen." Not because she ran the house single-handedly but because he honored her wisdom, her woman power, her guidance and common sense.)

(My mother, Muna, is not one to coddle or offer a shoulder for a long-term weep. This woman—mother of five, mentor to many, architect of her own sanctuary—is my prayer partner. Known for quoting spiritual mantras from Prophet Muhammad [PBUH], Joel Osteen, and Maya Angelou, my mother takes Spirit seriously.

Life, she says, grows us up. With her you may get a pat on your back but more often she offers a way to snap back; she leads you to water and stays till you drink.)

Muna, my Mo'Betta Mama, my mentor and wise woman

warrior: She read my four words and texted three trails out of my valley.

1. Comedy. "Put on a talent sho' wid da gurlz. Put on some music and dance. Have them read you a story . . . Talk to yourself. Talk urself out."
2. Culture and compassion. "Let your daughters see you as a strong blk woman who is finding her way to the north . . . You can't forget that you have passengers; you must be strong for them . . . Come on, Harriet [Tubman], choose freedom! Choose freedom!"
3. Code. "Remember moss grows on the north side of the trees. Smell your freedom, my sister."

Freedom? I text back: "What I'ma be free from again?"

My mama: "LOL. From negative self-defeating thoughts and actions. U r finding your way back to the real Tasneem."

Ahhh, the real Tasneem.

BAM! I got a spirited shakedown from my own mama. Just like I asked.

I couldn't even sleep that night thinking about the power of words, of prayer and fresh perspectives. I praised my grand inner compass, my GodVoice, my intuition, which knew who could help me redirect my thoughts.

And yet there I was, despite this wealth of wisdom, wallowing in the trenches of a melancholy mama moment. But, MMPH, Spirit provides. Every time.

When I was down, words—spoken, text, and remembered from the mouths of my mother—lifted me up.

Accept all situations, she said. Recognize the struggle. Slide into the valley, if you must. Moan, stew, thrash, rage, if you need. But, soon summon the Most High, the Creator, the One, Big Mama.

And you must listen—in whatever voice She chooses to speak through—listen to Her divine commands: Get up, lift your chin, open your eyes, cock your head, and rise, sweet sister! RISE!

Because you better believe, Mama always knows best.

THE REACH OF
A SMALL MOMENT

~~~~~~~~~~~~~~~

ALEXANDRA ROSAS

De la Sierra Morena
Cielito lindo, vienen bajando
Un par de ojitos negros
Cielito lindo, de contrabando

From the Sierra Morena
My beautiful sky, they come down
A pair of blackest eyes
Pretty little heaven, which I cannot have

sit cross-legged on the floor, holding the baby doll that my Spanish grandmother has bought me.

My grandmother sits behind me, singing softly as she patiently runs a wide-toothed comb, which she every now and then dips into a mason jar of warmed rhubarb water, through my jungle of curly, almost black hair. She takes the smallest section of my hair, wets it down with the rhubarb water, and then twists it into cork-screw curls, *cochumbos,* around her little finger.

She sings this song to me every morning—in a peaceful, wistful way.

"Be sure to smooth your hands over your baby doll, your *muñequita,*" my grandmother instructs me in Spanish as she finishes my hair. "You want her to feel safe." I immediately rub my hands over my baby doll's head, I want her to feel safe.

The beautiful, tall rhubarb that she grows in the middle of our yard is cut and boiled down to a thick, syrupy juice. Somehow, using it every day in my dark hair lightens my hair's color to a golden brown for the summer.

"Now, when you go outside to play in the sun and your hair dries, you'll have Shirley Temple rings," I hear her promise me in Spanish.

She uses the last of the rhubarb water, and I hear a clang as the blue comb that she uses every day on my hair hits the side of the jar. She asks me with her soft, slow voice to please help her up from the kitchen chair, if it's not too much trouble.

I am only four years old, and I have only known love at my grandmother's hand.

I help my grandmother stand and she laughs as she sees me pull her up with all my four-year-old might. She sings to me while she walks me to the mirror in the front hallway. We stop and stare at our reflection; she stands behind me. Reaching around from behind me, she holds my chin up gently with the tips of her pink manicured fingernails. I can tell she wants me to see myself. We say nothing, but I feel her looking at me. I look at myself, too.

"Those dark eyes!" She laughs. "You have such beautiful dark eyes. And the most delicious laugh. You are like a little doll, you are my *muñequita*."

I smile, too shy to look back at myself in the mirror. I finally look up and see what she sees, a little doll, all dark curls and round, dark eyes.

My grandmother and I stand together, in one reflection, while she moves her hands over my small shoulders. I feel so safe, and it makes me hug my doll tight.

She turns me around so that I face her, and I'm caught breathless as she gathers me so tightly inside her arms—the very way I'm holding my doll. Suddenly, all the ugliness of my world disappears.

There is always peace at my grandmother's hand, and in her arms. With my doll pressed against my chest, I close my eyes and bury my head deep in my grandmother's bosom. I want to stay there forever, with my eyes closed, my ears covered, all by her.

The morning above occurred in 1965, two years before my father committed suicide on Thanksgiving Day, when I had just begun first grade.

The morning above occurred during what would have been a typical day home with my clinically depressed mother, a day when my mother would not have been able to look at us, speak to us, or make eye contact with us.

As I write about this morning, about this small moment in my life, I can see from the distance of years the power a moment contains.

I still feel how my grandmother had me convinced that even though there were six of us born to my mother, it was I who was the special one, I who was the most loved one.

When my grandmother passed away, I had nowhere to turn with my grief. I confided in my siblings, seeking them out privately one by one, at her funeral. But they were as distraught as I was. We were overcome with the pain of our broken hearts, and whispered our confidences to each other. "You know, I was her favorite." Fools. How could my siblings be such fools and even think that? Clearly, it was I who was the favorite.

> *De la Sierra Morena*
> *Cielito lindo, vienen bajando*
> *Un par de ojitos negros*
> *Cielito lindo, de contrabando*

I am singing to my four-year-old son as I work my thick, green comb through the curly knots that are his hair. I begin to tell him that the song he hears is the same song my grandmother sang to me while she combed my hair when I was little.

In the middle of telling him this, I am hit by an impulse too strong and quick for me to stop and the urgency of my feelings makes me pull my son into me, grasping him in an embrace that I need more than he does.

"I love you, Mama," he somehow knows what to say. His muffled words rise up to me from my chest.

With an ache in my throat impossible to swallow away, I croak back, "I love you, too."

The power of the small moment that my grandmother created for me has carried me to this very moment here.

Did she know that while she sang and loved me, she was creating this small moment? I don't know. Did she know that I'd be writing of that morning, forty-five years later?

Would she have known the reach of a small moment?

The force of the memory of that morning with my grandmother makes me now stop and look at my beautiful children. With eye contact, with words heard and with words returned, with full, burying embraces—I want to give my children moments that will reach to the year 2050 and beyond.

BECOMING INVISIBLE

LEA GROVER

When my father was just a few months younger than I am now, he tried to throw my mother a surprise party.

She was turning thirty, and although she has never been the sort of person who particularly cares about that sort of thing, thirty is kind of a big deal. It signals a farewell to a specific kind of youth and identity, and as my six-months-younger father cared quite a bit about *that sort of thing*, he wanted to do something memorable.

He put a lot of work into the party. He invited dozens of people, all of whom were thrilled to come and celebrate my mom—who would never in a million years organize anything like it for herself. And he placed an order for a dozen cheesecakes, in a variety of flavors, to surprise his wife, who loved cheesecake. Their friends would bring food, potluck-style, their friends' children would play with me and my sisters, and my mother would experience a spectacular thirtieth birthday party.

That was his plan. But in the early spring of 1987, a terrible flu spread through the city of Pittsburgh. The morning of the party he collected the cheesecakes, and the phone calls started coming in. All but three guests, or their children, had started puking, and couldn't come. My father canceled the party, and he and my mother celebrated her thirtieth birthday quietly, packing as much cheesecake as they could into the freezer and living off the rest for weeks.

I was completely oblivious to these events. I was three years old, and my memory of my mother's thirtieth birthday is that my parents smiled a lot, that my sisters and I got My Little Ponies, and that the house was unusually clean.

Now I feel like I understand my parents. Why my father, at my age, would have wanted so badly to do something special. I understand why my mother, at my age, with three children the ages of my children, would buy *them* presents for *her* birthday. I understand how helpless my father must have felt to make one day, any day, about her. And I understand how much the gesture must have meant to my mother.

Now I get it.

When you stay at home all day, when your job is your children, life is only about you if something terrible happens. If you get very sick, or injured, if you lose a loved one. And that's why my memories of my mother's birthday involve a stuffed purple pony hopping on the dining room table.

As I near my thirtieth birthday, I think about this. I think about my father as he was then, barely thickening around the middle, wearing faded blue jeans and subversive T-shirts. I can see his wide smile, his deep dimples, his bright eyes. I can picture him at my age, just as clearly as I can picture him now.

But not my mother. I can picture the photographs of her, yes, but no matter how I rack my brain I can't see her as she was when she turned thirty years old.

I can see her hands, rolling cookie dough into balls, dropping them gracefully onto a pan. I can see her wedding ring clear as day, and her fingernails, and her wrists.

I can see the backs of her jeans as she walks ahead of me down the sidewalk, the tail of her shirt hiding her back pocket as she pulls out her wallet to give me money for the ice cream truck.

I can see her bare legs in front of her on the porch floor, her ankles crossed and a train of ants walking across them. They look like my legs.

I can see her silhouette at the bottom of the stairs, casually warning me to give up my attempts to somersault down to the living room.

I can see the barrette in the back of her hair as she sits at the table.

But I can't see her face. I cannot assemble these pieces. My mother is an invisible force of nature, a supernatural entity made of love and discipline and constant presence.

I looked at my father. I studied him, this person I loved, who lived with me but whose comings and goings from a mysterious place called "work" carried the weight of disappearances and reinvention.

I never had to look at my mother. I was always confident that she was there.

At thirty years old, my mother was invisible to me. She will always be something of a mystery. No matter how closely my family parallels hers, no matter how similar our struggles and joys and the mundane details of our lives, no matter how much I understand her as she is now, I will never be able to put my feet into her shoes and sympathize with her life the way I do my father's.

And in a way, this makes me feel closer to every mother. To every other woman who has been a shadow, an omnipresent force in her children's lives.

I am this vibration, this mysterious force. And in my own ethereal, faceless way, I will also be erased from my children's memories, continuously replaced by the constantly changing, constantly aging face before them.

In my memories, if I must picture my mother, I see her now. Maybe a little less gray, maybe somewhat thinner, but still—as she is now. That girl, that young woman, she is somebody I will never know.

I feel the grief that I have already lost part of my mother forever.

I see it in my own children, who once stared forever at me unblinking as they lay swaddled in my arms, and now run past without so much as a glance when I remind them to wash their hands or hang up their coats.

Maybe it isn't turning thirty that bothers me. Maybe it's losing myself in motherhood. Maybe it's the fear that I'm already gone, replaced by this ghost whose voice will soothe my children's memories, long after I've died.

And while I mourn this former me, I am filled with a guilt and a joy so great they bring me to tears. I have always wanted to be this thing, immortal and benevolent and profoundly loved. Loved until I dissolved into the enormity of the word, until it absorbed me and replaced me with the all-powerful phantom caring for every child, every person, with a fierceness so raw and so bold and yet so constant that they disappeared into it.

I have always wanted to be a mom.

MOTHERHOOD OFF THE BEATEN PATH

MARGARET SMITH

D r. Kornfeld, my fertility doctor, came highly recommended. Her success rate was unequaled. Except that doctor who was arrested for inseminating his patients with his own sperm. And you know those mothers wouldn't have pressed charges if he had the good fortune to look like Brad Pitt. But it was his lot in life to look like, albeit with thick black hair, SpongeBob. It's guys like him who are endowed with Olympian sperm. Their sperm is genetically encoded to succeed. It has evolved to compensate for looks. In other words, it knows it's only getting one chance, so it could bounce off a wall onto a woman's thigh and army-crawl its way to her vagina. Brad Pitt, on the other hand, doesn't even have to have sperm. Dust could puff out and he'd still do well.

Dr. Kornfeld came into the room with my folder. "Your levels look great. You're very young reproductively." I liked her immediately. She informed me of my options for donors, including specimens right there in her office. Patients who had become pregnant and didn't need them anymore left their extras in her care. It made sense that you couldn't return the stuff, what with all the product tampering that goes on. This sperm was appealing. It had a good track record. But I didn't like the fact that my child could be in the same school district with an unknown sibling. They could meet, fall in love, and then find out the awful truth. You've watched Lifetime Channel. I decided the California Cryobank made the most sense. It wasn't far from my house. I could pick it up myself, bring it to Kornfeld's office, and save a few dollars. My mother might start to warm to the idea of my inseminating if I could tell her I got a deal.

Dr. Kornfeld told me two things on my way out of her office that day: "I'm not gay but I'd jump the fence for Ellen," and, "My worst donor nightmare would be sperm with a Kevin Bacon nose." I said, "Too bad none of these places offer pictures." What she said next changed everything. "Oh, there is a place in Georgia that's doing that now. They just sent me some literature." Cherubs came from behind clouds with harps and sang songs. What was once impossible was now possible. The world was smiling upon me and the Universe was saying "cheese."

I called the firm in Augusta on my way home and requested their donor list. A few days later it arrived: five pages of Mr. Rights. Each candidate had a number and nine columns of description: ethnic origin, hair color, eye color, skin tone, blood type, body type, occupation, and interests/religion. A number sign meant a photo was available. I scanned the list for pound signs. There was one, then another and another. They all had straight hair. I wanted curly. Straight hair, straight hair, straight hair, straight thinning hair. What is going on? Then I saw it: a number sign with brown curly hair, blue eyes, fair skin, six foot one, 190 pounds, occupation electric company. Not exactly an occupation, but he could be an engineer or maybe he touched some bare wires and has a nice desk job now. Then I noticed the interest/religion column, fishing, hunting, baseball, and THE CHURCH OF GOD. I don't know about you but I can't read the words CHURCH OF GOD without hearing it in a deep fire-and-brimstone voice. CHURCH OF GOD!

I didn't want Churchy sperm. My lower self was rearing its head. It takes very little sometimes to send me into a downward spiral. This one went like this: "I can't believe I have to ask someone for sperm, let alone pay for it. Two hundred seventy-five dollars a batch? Was it cheaper in college or what? I was practically tripping over the stuff. Now look at me calling out of state for some and begging for a picture. I'm pathetic." I was trying to experience a person based on a few facts written on a piece of paper. Who is donor 666 without the distraction of a flirtatious comment or a crooked smile to animate his DNA?

"Hi, I'm calling about donor 9059." She said, "Well, let's see." I could hear her shuffling papers. I said, "I have the list, it says he comes with a picture." I immediately had this fantasy of her saying, "Well, if you put it that way, they all come with a picture, don't they?" But that's not what she said. What she said was "We're out of 9059." I had never even considered the possibility of rejection. Here I was vulnerable, unsuspecting, and boom, a big fat NO. She could have at least asked me if I was sitting down. "There's none left," I said in a pathetic Kübler-Ross first stage of grieving voice. "Yes, it's been discontinued."

I hurried into another stage of grieving, anger. "Sounds to me like the old bait and switch. It's on your list, but you're not getting any more?" "That is correct." I was now in the final stage, acceptance. Surrender always puts me in touch with my higher self. Now I wanted to be nice to her. Did we not both suffer? On some level I guess I thought we were in the same boat. I didn't have any sperm and now I saw that she was capable of running out, too.

I said, "I have a couple others circled that look interesting." I was on the rebound. The donors had become just "interesting." I would probably never get so attached to another. "What about 92-76?" "No, we're out of that." "How about 96-20, thinning hair, you must have a barrel full of that." "I'm afraid we're out of that, too." There wasn't a bit of regret in her voice. "If you're out of everything," I asked, "why bother to answer the phone?" Silence. "Will that be all?"

I had a good feeling about one last donor. "What about 8801?" He was premed, English/Irish decent. She said, "We don't have any left in the regular, but we have some in the Blue Line Special."

I flipped through my pages. Had I missed something in my desperation? I didn't see anything about a special. How would I tell my mother that I had missed the special? "What's the Blue Line Special?" She said, "Well, a regular specimen has about fifty thousand spermatazoa, the Blue Line has over one hundred thousand. It is a bit more expensive but you're getting twice the count." I knew from going to Starbucks that a double shot cost more. I felt drained. I needed to hang up at that point. I didn't know how special the special really was and no way was I prepared to say, "No thanks, give me the cheap stuff." I hung up and called my mother because I wanted to end my day on an even lower note. I told her the experience I had on the phone with the sperm bank.

She said, "I don't know why you can't get pregnant like your sisters and I did."

I said, "Because I don't like the taste of gin."

THE JOB OF MOTHERHOOD

~~~~~~~~~~~~

WENDI AARONS

It's been said that motherhood is the toughest job in the world. And that is complete bullshit.

I'm sorry, but I have to totally disagree with Oprah on this one. Yeah, I said it. *Oprah is wrong.* (Why do I suddenly feel like Gayle King is parked outside my house in an unmarked van?) But I stand by what I said—motherhood isn't the toughest job in the world. What about astronaut? Or neurologist? Or the guy who shampoos Elton John's wigs and/or merkins? Those are hard jobs. We mothers can sprawl on the couch drinking white wine and watching *The Wonder Pets* all day. Not that I do that, of course. Anymore.

But what most mothers don't realize is that your life actually becomes *easier* once you have children.

For example: Before kids, it can be challenging to come up with excuses to get out of boring social obligations. Trust me, there are only *so* many times you can cry food poisoning before your boss figures out that the only thing making you puke is the thought of seeing him in a Speedo at his pool party.

But once you have kids, finding excuses is a no-brainer.

"Sorry, can't make your wedding! Colton has explosive diarrhea!"

"Sorry, have to pass on your Pampered Chef party. Amelia has a project due!"

"Sorry, can't give that grand jury testimony today, Senator. We have LICE."

Yeah, that's right. Lice is the mother of all excuses. It will get you out of absolutely anything. I've falsely claimed we've had lice so many times, I'm surprised the Centers for Disease Control hasn't shown up at our house with a dump truck full of de-licing powder. And SEAL Team Six to rub it all over our heads.

Yet another way kids make Mom's life easier is that you can finally let go of all your crazy hopes and dreams and just live vicariously through your children. If you always wanted to be a dancer but never made it to Broadway, sign your daughter up for ballet. If you never became a movie star, get your son into acting. No gold medal for downhill skiing? Push that little scamp of yours down a black diamond run. Of course, most of the mothers I know still accomplish many amazing things on their own, but honestly. Why work so hard when you don't have to? If the moms on *Toddlers & Tiaras* have taught us anything, it's that we should all just relax, put up our feet, and spray-tan the hell out of a six-year-old. Easy!

A woman's life also becomes less demanding when she's a mother because she can finally give up in the old looks department. This starts with pregnancy, when your stomach grows and grows and you turn into a sweaty bowling ball with legs. Of course, your friends will tell you that you look "radiant" and "glowing" and "beautiful." But come on, that's just so you don't sit on them.

Then, once you have the baby, well, let's just say if you told people you'd recently escaped from the Oklahoma State Women's Prison, no one would argue. Because things are not pretty. Not pretty at all. And by "things," I mean your ass. Sorry, mama, but it's true.

Because the post-baby body is Chernobyl. Your boobs leak, your hair falls out, and you're covered in so much spit-up that when it's dark, you glow green like a radioactive alien. Although maybe that was just me. I did grow up near the Nevada nuclear test site.

But the good news is when you're a mom, you spend most of your time with little people who don't care what you look like when they're begging you for snacks. And that's great because then you don't have to worry about the latest trends. Or the latest styles. Or whether or not your hair is "washed." The wonderful thing about kids is that they all think their mommy is beautiful, no matter what. Husbands, well, that's a different story and you'll probably see it on the Lifetime Movie Network. But we moms can just let it all hang out and be comfortable in our sweatshirts—and yoga pants. (Seriously, does every woman on the planet only wear yoga pants now? If all of the moms I know who wear yoga pants actually *did* yoga, our PTO meetings would be a lot less nasty. Nobody throws punches after a few *namaste*s.)

Finally the last, but perhaps the best, way motherhood makes your life easier is if and when you ever get pulled over for speeding, like say, sixty miles per hour in a school zone, you can always get out of the ticket by telling the officer that you're only in a hurry because your baby has colic. Even if your baby is eighteen and currently serving in the United States armed forces. Works every damn time.

So the next time you hear someone complain about how tough motherhood is, please. For my sake, don't believe them. Especially if they have lice.

NOT A PRINCESS

~~~~~~

VIKKI REICH

My daughter is not a princess.

She hates pink. She doesn't like things that sparkle and has no interest in dresses or skirts, in flowers and lace.

She wears dark blue skinny jeans and a teal shirt emblazoned with a *Tyrannosaurus rex* in sunglasses playing an electric guitar. She covers her messy, short brown hair with a black and gray stocking cap, and her favorite shoes are high-tops that are a vibrant mix of black and blue, yellow and orange.

My daughter is a wannabe rock star and she is often mistaken for a boy.

She has always been deliberate in the way she dresses, has always chosen her own clothes, and we have followed her many fashion whims, but she didn't always dress as she does now.

Shortly after she turned five, we were invited to a formal cocktail party and she chose a white satin dress, the bottom of which was layered in tulle and embroidered with tiny pink flowers. She picked out a pink sweater and patent leather Mary Janes to complete the look.

But in the months following that party, her style slowly began to change.

She started pairing her skirts with T-shirts and her brother's ties. There was a brief period during which she was fascinated with bow ties. Soon after that, she replaced her skirts with jeans and cargo shorts.

On the day of her kindergarten picture, she bounded down the stairs wearing her brother's pink oxford dress shirt, his black-and-gray-plaid vest, and a pair of black velvet pants. Her smile exuded joy and confidence and I should have taken that as a sign that we were doing something right.

I should have felt proud.

But I didn't. I wanted to cry. I wanted to put her in a little pink dress and help her with her tights and buckle her patent leather shoes. I wanted to braid her hair or put in the colorful barrettes she used to love so much.

I wanted her to look like all the other little girls her age.

It would be easy for me to appear noble. I could tell you that I didn't want her to have to deal with the experience of feeling different, that I didn't want her to be teased. But I would be lying.

The truth is that I worried what people would think about me.

We hear it constantly from the media and politicians: Children of queer parents will turn out to be queer themselves. Children without both a mother and a father will become confused about gender. This is the abstract context in which families like mine exist. But it is not just abstraction.

A couple of months after school pictures were taken, the parents from my daughter's class got together for a potluck. The class photo sat on a table and twenty-eight kids stared out from that picture—boys in jeans and T-shirts, girls in dresses or pastel-colored pants, and our daughter in her black velvet pants and vest.

My partner and I were standing in the kitchen with several parents who were poring over the picture and one of the mothers pointed to our daughter, laughed, and said to me, "Did you make her dress like that?!"

There was only one reason she would make that assumption. I tried to breathe evenly and told myself to keep it light.

"No. I didn't make her dress that way. You know I could never make her do anything."

The truth is that, even if I could, I wouldn't. But people don't know that. They don't know me or my partner or our daughter, and assumptions are easy to make.

Late at night, when the homework is done and the children have had their baths and they are tucked into bed and asleep at last, the house falls silent and I am alone with my doubts. In those moments, I am not the outspoken advocate for families like mine. I am not the feminist who defends her children's rights to express themselves in any way they choose. I am just a mother. And I worry.

Will they be happy? Will they be loved? Will they be kind and compassionate? And the pulse that races beneath each of those questions is "Are we good parents?" and I can't help but wonder by whose standards we will be judged.

I do not have the luxury of being simply a mother. I am and will always be a lesbian mother.

The truth is that it was easier when my daughter twirled through the world in skirts, when her hair was long and held back from her face in pigtails or braids. It was easier because I could point to her and say to the world, "See? She is just like every other girl. She is not like me."

But that is no longer true.

She is a lot like me and that is both beautiful and complicated and I want the same thing for both of us—to be seen in all our complexity.

One evening, my daughter was talking about a girl at school and said, "She thinks she's Rapunzel or Cinderella or something." She said it like it was an indictment of the girl's character and I thought she might want a character with whom she could identify, so I suggested that she might be more like a prince. She rolled her eyes and said, "Mom, I am not a prince. Obviously, I would be the king."

Those moments are the ones that matter, the moments that tell me everything I need to know about our endeavors as parents. It is not easy to be a girl in this world. It is not easy to be different and yet our daughter stubbornly remains true to herself.

My daughter is not a princess and believes that she can be anyone she wants to be. She is happy and loved and kind and compassionate.

That is more than enough.

THREADS

～～～～～～

STACEY CONNER

The commentary is always the same and I know that it will find me. At preschool pickup. In the checkout line.

There is no return policy. Children are not dogs. Adoption is for life. Did she think it would be easy? How dare she? Awful. Selfish.

What part of "forever" don't these horrible people who adopt children and give up understand? What part of "parent" don't they understand?

No part. I understand too well. I understand parenting one child to the trauma and detriment of another. I understand choosing between the needs of one child and another.

How could I give up?

I will try and paint it for you. If you will try to keep in mind that I am shaking as I write, four long years later.

The sun shone in the windows and, for the first time in two months, I felt a fragile peace. My traumatized, institutionalized five-year-old son with valid grief, with understandable rage and abandonment issues, actually leaned against me to see the story that I read. The tentative, warm touch of his arm against mine made it difficult for me to focus on the words. He had chosen to touch me. Months of screaming tantrums set off by nothing and rages and incidents with our fourteen-month-old daughter and twelve-month-old son that I tried to ignore faded away, melted into nothing at my feet. I could do this. I could do it if we could have these moments. If I could see the progress. If I could have something to give me hope that I was on the right track and he might someday love me and trust me enough that I could breathe.

My one-year-old son, my healthy, untraumatized child, toddled back and forth from the bookshelf to us, carrying offerings. He asked to sit in my lap and I pulled him up, but he cried and fussed and I set him down. He leaned against me from the floor and then started to cry and crawled away. Maybe eight or ten times, until I wondered if he was sick, but the fragile bond with my oldest boy held, and so when the baby found a quiet game to play on the far side of the room, I read books and snuggled with him as long as I could.

Shadows fell. I kissed my son and got up to start the evening routine. I sat on the ground to change the baby's diaper, pulled off his pants and pushed up his shirt. Angry red welts scattered across his stomach. One on his side. One on his back. My heart leaped to my throat. An allergic reaction? Hives? They weren't raised. They weren't itchy. In the middle they looked bruised.

I knew, then. I looked up and met my oldest son's eyes and I knew. The hard, angry, heartbreakingly familiar set of his face. Defiant, daring, asking. What are you going to do now? Do you still want to be my mother now? The price for my peace. The price for my oblivion and my quiet and my desperate need to have everything work for just one afternoon. I could see my older son's rage splashed in vivid red on my baby's stomach.

I could see the price and it was too high for me. I knew he needed to learn that he would be loved no matter what. *Trauma, anger, grief,* some part of my brain whispered to whatever small part of me remembered to be his mother. *I know. I know. I know.* I knew and I still shook with rage at a five-year-old boy. There's no easier way to say it. *I shook with rage at a five-year-old boy.*

I took his hand and he writhed and screamed and fought and bit and scratched and I don't blame him. Pure survival instincts. He sensed the danger as well as I did. I pulled him up the stairs as gently but quickly as I could, protecting myself as best I could and I put him in his room and I locked the door.

It wasn't to keep him in. It wasn't to contain his tantrum, which raged inside, turning over furniture and ripping apart bedding and kicking and screaming.

I didn't lock the door to keep him in.

I turned the lock because I didn't think I could open a locked door to hurt a child.

And I didn't. But I wanted to. I wanted to go in there and spank him until I couldn't lift my arm. I wanted to hold him down and hurt him like he hurt my baby.

I stood on the other side of the door with my head against it and all my education, all my love, all my good intentions, all my reading, all my preparation, the time with the social workers, the words of the attachment therapist were nothing. Nothing. There was nothing and no one there to help me and I have never been so angry, so on the edge of out of control, in my life.

That's where we are, these parents the world condemns. That

is what the bottom looks like. Imagine that you stand at the top of a dark well, looking down at a parent, sitting at the bottom with her head on her knees. Would you try to throw her a rope or would you spit on her? Which do you think helps the child?

I will tell you what helped my children. A family that wanted a child. A family with only teenagers. A family that had parented traumatized, reactive attachment disorder children before. A mother who, on the day that my oldest child became hers, said to me not only, "We can do this; it's okay to let go," but also, "We understand why you can't."

They didn't throw me a rope, they built my whole family a staircase and it was in the best interest of every single one of my children, my oldest son most of all.

What can we do to help? What can we offer in the place of judgment, instead of scathing commentary? *We* don't have to be the whole rope. All we have to be is a thread.

It is a painful reality that a child can be so damaged in the first few years of life that he becomes a terrifying and heart-breaking impossibility for the parents who have opened their hearts and their homes to try to love him. But each and every one of us can be a thread in the rope for change and healing.

How about this? The next time you see a mom "with a horrible kid" "losing it" at the playground, take a deep breath and instead of commenting on the "terrible parent doing nothing while her daughter screams," think:

Maybe this is the twentieth tantrum today.

Maybe she was up all night.

Maybe the situation is ten million times more complicated than I realize.

And then meet that mother's eyes and smile at her.

Because maybe, just maybe, an hour ago, she walked away from that child's door. And maybe, just maybe, for the cost of a smile, you gave her the strength to do it again.

Just like that, you're a thread in the rope. Now we're helping children.

SHE KNEW IT

~~~~~~~~~~

NATALIE CHEUNG HALL

never knew you could make millions from writing a book about how Chinese moms are pushy until I heard about that "Tiger Mom" business. I could have been a millionaire. Instead, I'm just a run-of-the-mill Chinese-American mom with a run-of-the-mill pushy Chinese mom.

My mother was a fan of brevity and tough love, and she had an answer for whatever life entailed. When I was nervous before trying out for the cross-country team, she said, "I knew it—you didn't practice run enough!" but when I made the team, it was "I knew it whole time—you are good runner!" When I was nervous about college acceptances, she said, "I knew it—remember that time two year ago when you sneaky watch TV? You are lazy!" but when I got into all the schools I applied to, it was "I knew it whole time! You are the smart!" When I lamented the lack of a love life, she said, "I knew it! How many times I tell you—NO man want a woman who wears ponytail?!" but when I started a relationship: "I knew it whole time! You are a catch!" This woman seriously knew *everything*.

This clairvoyance lasted through my college years and then the "dark year" when I did not immediately enter graduate school. Things were not looking up for me and she knew it—I mean, I was still defiantly sporting a ponytail. But I learned to find the fact that she ended every phone conversation with me with "Your life in toilet!" humorous, because the minute I did anything that made me proud, she was standing right there next to me, ready to tell the world, "I knew it whole time, that's my girl!"

My life began to fill out: I finished graduate school, began a career, met a nice young man with a PhD, and we were engaged. When times were rough, moving far from home and later battling with infertility, she harshly put me in my place, but was also the first to vigorously congratulate me when I triumphed. I enjoyed many nice years of positive "I knew its" when I got promoted, finished races, got pregnant, and was enjoying the security and partnership of marriage. I, too, slowly began to "know" that I could do this whole "life" thing. I made a decision to be motivated with the disappointed "I knew its" and believed her when she knew I would succeed.

However, after the birth of my son, things changed again. I dwelled on the failure of my beautifully crafted birth plan when my natural birth turned into a C-section. People would come to see the new life we created, and I would find myself cornering anyone who would listen, detailing my fruitless labor that landed me on the operating table, shaking too much from weakness and drugs to even hold him when they pulled him out. I booked appointments with my OB, countless lactation consultants, a breast surgeon when breast-feeding was not working.

I begged for a diagnosis: thrush, yeast infection, clogged duct—anything that could be remedied by smearing indigo all over my nipples. Soon, not only could I not stomach breast-feeding, but the touch of my son made me want to crawl into my own skin. I wallowed in the smell of formula when breast-feeding failed altogether, and I told myself I could barely be considered a mother when he stayed sick that entire winter; I knew it was directly correlated to not breast-feeding.

I was in the throes of postpartum depression, and I had nowhere to turn. Things got worse. My marriage failed. More accurately: I failed my marriage, my husband. I moved from my sunny home into a stale apartment with a one-year-old, where the worn walls and carpet made me second-guess my choice. I felt paralyzed by all the fear, insecurity, and stress that define single parenting.

What did my mom say then? She didn't say anything because I did not open up to her. I could not bear to hear she had a failure for a daughter. I already "knew it"; she didn't have to tell me this time. I was broken, I was embarrassed, I was ashamed.

Then one day, while my mom was visiting for the first time in my apartment, I could feel her watching me with my son. My whole body got hot and sticky; I steeled myself for her biting commentary. Instead, she did what she did best—she gave me what I needed. She said, "He is pure joy, it reminds me of you. He is so happy; he is going to be just fine. I always knew you would be a wonderful mother. I knew it whole time." I don't know if she knew it that day, but she knew what I needed. She knew she had the power to give me strength, and she chose to give it to me.

Now I know it, too. I am a good mom because I have a good mom.

And that's why you should listen to your mother. Because she knew it the whole time.

PEANUT BUTTER AND JELLY

~~~~~~~~~~

TAYA DUNN JOHNSON

In my world, motherhood and fatherhood go hand in hand, kind of like peanut butter and jelly. I was raised by my married parents, all my aunts and uncles were married, and marriage was all I knew growing up.

Things in my life proceeded in the way that I felt they should.

I fell in love with my high school sweetheart. We fit together just like peanut butter and jelly.

We dated.

We went to college.

We got married.

We bought a house.

We decided together to start a family.

We had a son.

Then my husband died.

And my perception of motherhood changed.

Back in 2008, the moment that my husband and I found out I was carrying a baby boy, we experienced a set of emotions that we couldn't voice. Tremendous joy on the surface, but something else was there. I had secretly prayed for a boy, thinking I'd not be able to handle a *prissy, frilly, pink, emotional little lady*. I had been a tomboy nerd, so I thought that being the mom to a boy would be *perfect*. Of course, I welcomed whatever child we would be blessed with, but secretly, yep, I wanted a boy. My husband would later say that he was secretly pulling for a boy as well. However, our joy of the moment was tempered by the reality. We, an African American couple, would be bringing a little black boy into the world. The magnitude of that conclusion nearly took our breaths away. Although this was September of 2008, I remember the moment as if it were yesterday. Our eyes locked over the head of my perinatologist and I saw every emotion that I was feeling reflected in his eyes. We didn't discuss "it" for a couple of weeks. We pushed it to the backs of our minds as we happily attended several baby showers in our honor, tried to agree on a name, and basked in the general happiness.

Late one night, as my husband was rubbing my expanding belly, he began to cry. He spoke to the new responsibility that we were undertaking. Welcoming a child to this world is both beautiful and terrifying. And our fear was doubled, as raising an African American boy presents a unique set of challenges and concerns. Although this country has made great strides in regard to race relations, racism and discrimination still exist. And unfortunately, much of that which bubbles under the surface—anger, fear, ignorance, and hatred—is often directed at and acted upon black boys and men. One saving grace from our conversation was the fact that we were a family and my husband would be *present* to raise our boy into a man. That gave me great comfort.

Our joy, Marcus, was born January 13, 2009, and he is the spitting image of his father. At the age of two, Marcus was diagnosed on the autism spectrum. Parenting our son for three and a half years was amazing. Every day as we watched him grow and develop, we embraced the little moments. We each relished our roles as mother and father. We loved and parented in two very different ways and the partnership worked wonderfully, just like peanut butter and jelly.

Then, on June 9 of 2012, my world shattered and my peace vanished. My husband passed away unexpectedly from a massive heart attack. Peanut butter with no jelly is hard as hell to swallow. Not only was I a widow at the age of thirty-five, but I was left here to parent alone. I am a widowed mother to a little black boy with special needs. Each passing day, I must temper my grief and try to remain gentle with myself while attempting to be as "in the moment" as I can with our son. I am his mother and I must do everything within my power to instill in him the tools he needs to grow, thrive, and flourish.

Motherhood means that I must give of myself unselfishly while putting every ounce of love that I have into our son. Motherhood means that I must surround our son with uncles, cousins, and male family friends so that he will understand the kind of man his father was and the kind of man that we expect him to become. Motherhood means that in this moment, I don't have a partner or a physical father for our son but I must make sure that Marcus does not suffer from this absence. Motherhood is my charge and I have accepted the call.

THE GOOD-BYE APP

KATE ST. VINCENT VOGL

We start with the letting go. The hardest part.

This part takes place in southern Virginia, at the College of William and Mary, where we unpacked a minivan and carried a year's worth of possessions up the steps of a one-hundred-year-old building and down a long hall, into a room taller than it was wide. Air-conditioning? In Virginia? Did I mention this was a one-hundred-year-old building?

After the day of moving in, stretching extra-long pink sheets onto a lofted bed, and driving around to find a Target that still carried the right-sized window fan, we spent the night in Williamsburg for the welcome celebration. We gathered along with thousands of others on the lawn of the palace gardens to watch fireworks. It was momentous, it was beautiful, it was without our daughter. She was there, somewhere near us, at least according to Find My Friend on my iPhone.

We never did find her. The fife and drum corps started up, and we followed them and the torches the whole way down Duke of Gloucester Street, not willing to fall behind because we could not stand the thought of not seeing her on this part of the journey. But we never saw her there, either.

We staked ourselves by the historical home of the college president, not willing to give up any ground when they said parents should step back, step back. We watched the freshmen advance, flags of their dorms waving. Monroe Hall, Hunt Row, *that's her, that's her!* We strained to see her, to listen for her voice as the students serenaded the president. We never did hear her.

We hurried back to her dorm and hovered in the shadows near the steps. And there, we saw her striding across the lawn, between others. Under an arc of campus light, we saw she was okay, already with friends. "That's her," we whispered to each other. "That's her."

She came to us, already changed. Eyes bright as the middle August moon. Smile quick. All that I'd hoped for her, it was here. We said our good-byes. We went back to our hotel with a hole in our family.

The next morning, we resolved to attend the rest of the parent orientation sessions. We pulled out our maps and opened umbrellas and began our walk. In planning out the trip, we thought we'd have this part of the day with our daughter, too, and we didn't. It was a long walk to the conference center. We'd walked a mile and my husband said, "It's still farther." The light rain turned spiteful. Rain soaked my pants to the knee. "It's still farther." We crossed against the light, set our jaws. We were Midwesterners, we could do this.

That little spite in the rain turned into a campus crusade, a deluge. We ducked under the awning of a Days Inn. My iPhone said we'd walked two miles out of our way. My husband wanted a cab, but by the time it would come, the session would be over. We could just walk back to it.

On the way back, there were rivers to forge through, but I'm told I speak in hyperboles. I was wet to my hips now—this was not hyperbole. We got all the way back to where my phone said we should be, and I realized I'd plugged in the general campus address. We'd actually been on the right track before, back by the Days Inn.

We changed plans, trudged back to the hotel. We dried off. Changed clothes. Checked out. And *drove* to the session. Turned out, we didn't need it. It was for parents who couldn't let go.

We'd walked clear past any such needs.

We drove off campus without saying another good-bye. I sent a text and turned off my Find My Friend app for my daughter. I knew what I needed to know. She was there. I was somewhere else, on a Virginia highway, stuck in traffic.

This was the time for gathering ourselves together.

What these currents of life bring, what they take away, it's changing, constantly changing. All we can do is keep crossing that bridge to reach the others around us. Sometimes the weight of what we carry across can feel overwhelming. Sometimes we're too fearful of what's sweeping past, too worried about our footing to see what's on the other side.

Letting go might be hardest, but that's not what lasts.

MORE THAN AN AUNT,
LESS THAN A MOM

~~~~~~~~~~~~~~~~

JERRY MAHONEY

There are plenty of responses you expect to get when you tell your loved ones you're starting a family. "How exciting!" or "You're going to be amazing parents!" or just a simple "Congratulations!" The one I remember the most, though, was "That's fucked up!"

It was my brother-in-law Peter who said it, and to be fair, what we were proposing was a little different from how the school nurse tells you babies are made when you're in fourth grade. Given that my husband and I are both men, though, our options weren't exactly covered in elementary school health class. When Drew, my husband, and I first started thinking about becoming dads, we focused on adoption, as many gay men do. We quickly learned what a long, difficult road that would be, and we decided to go a different way—gestational surrogacy. We had an agency finding us a woman who would carry our child, and we had another woman who'd agreed to be our egg donor. That's the part Peter wasn't crazy about.

Drew and I had struggled for weeks to pick just the right woman, scouring websites full of strangers willing to entwine their DNA with ours. There were so many possibilities, and yet nothing we both agreed on. Perhaps it was the limited information available on these women, the fact that some of the candidates were as young as nineteen, or the fees, which ranged from $8,000 to $30,000, the pricier ones being the Harvard-educated blondes. Just as we were struggling with how to navigate this personal and ethical minefield, the perfect egg donor showed up unexpectedly on Drew's caller ID.

"You know you can have my eggs if you want them, right?" she said. It was that swift, that casual. Something we'd quietly debated for months, she blurted out in an instant on a long-distance phone call. "You can have my eggs if you want them," as if she were offering to loan us her hair dryer or Ani DiFranco CDs, rather than a part of her womanhood.

"I have to go. I'll call you later." Drew hung up, stunned.

"Who was that?" I asked.

"My sister, Susie," Drew said. "She just offered us her eggs."

Susie was also Peter's sister, and that was the problem. Sure, using Susie's eggs would mean I would provide the sperm. That way we wouldn't end up with some inbred, three-headed freak baby. But that didn't totally erase the potential for weirdness. None of us knew exactly what kind of family we'd have at the end of this. What would Susie be to this kid? An aunt? A mommy? Both?

Only a few minutes later, an e-mail arrived. "I was serious about supplying eggs," Susie wrote. "And it would be a matter of me handing the eggs over and washing my hands of the situation.

And if for some reason the kid turns out unattractive, we could blame that loser egg donor that nobody knows."

As complicated as the idea might be, the advantages were too big to overlook. Susie had everything we wanted in an egg donor. She was smart, beautiful, a talented artist, and most of all, had the biggest heart of anyone we knew, which was only made more obvious by her latest offer. On top of it all, Drew and I loved the idea of creating a child who would be genetically linked to both of us. We might see my nose on our child's face or Drew's ears. Would it haunt us if we also saw Susie's smile?

Perhaps more important, would it haunt Susie? She was young and unattached. She wanted kids of her own someday, just not now. But this would be our kid, not hers. Right? Would she be okay if her brother had a baby with her DNA whom she was only an aunt to? We decided to fly her out to California, where we lived, to find out.

We were eager for Susie to meet our fertility doctor, a jovial middle-aged man named Dr. Saroyan, whom we'd grown especially fond of. We admired his honesty and his expertise. Drew and I waited while he gave Susie an ultrasound, and then he sat the three of us down to share the results.

"Your ovaries are perfect," he began. "You have beautiful, beautiful follicles. You are perfectly ready to make babies, but are you sure you want to do it for these guys?"

One other thing we loved about Dr. S was his dickish sense of humor.

"I mean, you could do a lot better than them," he went on.

"Yeah, but he's my brother," Susie played along. "I kind of have to."

With a plaster replica of the female reproductive system and a tiny wand, Dr. S explained to Susie exactly what she was signing up for. To get her body to produce enough eggs, Susie would have to take hormones. A lot of them. And they had to be injected. By her. In her butt. The side effects could include nausea, abdominal pain, and general moodiness.

"How bad are the injections?" I asked.

"I've never had anyone drop out because of the drugs," Dr. S assured. "But it's a pain in the ass."

Susie only had one question herself: "When do we start?"

Dr. S smiled, then he leaned in for a rare moment of seriousness. "What you're doing for your brother is a beautiful thing, Susan, and you are clearly a very special person. I'm going to take good care of you."

While Susie was at the fertility clinic, a nurse took a blood sample to test for genetic diseases. The only hurdle left was making sure Susie and I weren't predisposed to any of the same horrendous maladies.

Well, there was one other hurdle, too—Mindy, the therapist we took Susie to see.

"So what do you expect out of this arrangement?"

Susie shifted in her seat across from Mindy. "I just want to make my brothers happy."

By this point, Susie had talked to so many people about donating her eggs that she stayed composed and confident through even the toughest queries.

"It'll be their kid, not mine."

"I'm not ready to have a kid. But I'm ready to be an aunt."

"Because I love them. They're my brothers."

Susie aced the interrogation, but Mindy was suspicious. She started digging deeper.

"Why is it you never learned to drive?"

"I guess I just don't want to grow up," Susie confessed.

"Really? Because this is a very grown-up thing you're doing for Drew and Jerry."

Pretty soon after that, the Kleenex came out. Susie was an amazing woman, everything we wanted our kids to be, but like everyone, she had her baggage. Broken dreams, deep-seated insecurities, and lots of pain she generally preferred not to talk about.

Mindy had the right idea. If we wanted to be sure Susie was doing the right thing, we had to play hardball.

"We're going to need boundaries," I said, "and we should talk about them. Susie will be more than an aunt, but less than a mom. I love you, Susie, but if we have this kid, you're going to have to watch us make a lot of mistakes and know that you don't get a say in it. We'll decide where he goes to school, what she wears, whether we circumcise, how to discipline, what to buy them for Christmas, all the billion decisions parents have to make. And you're not going to like everything we do. We'll probably screw this kid up a million different ways, but they'll be our million ways."

All I wanted was for Mindy to give us her thumbs-up, but as the clock ticked away and our session came to an end, she conspicuously avoided saying yes. She didn't say no, either, which was just as frustrating.

What she said was that it would be complicated. Forever. We were entering into a gray area. Like our surrogacy agency had told us, we were pioneers. Sometimes pioneers got lost.

On our way home from the appointment, we were more confused than ever. That's when Peter called—for Susie. They talked for a long time. He asked her questions even tougher than the ones Mindy had asked. He knew just what to say, because he knew Susie so well. She cried some more. We waited anxiously to get his reaction. "I think what you're doing is pretty cool," he said, finally. "I'm really happy for all of you."

I realized that other people might share Peter's initial response. There would always be strangers who would think our situation was a bit fucked up. But that didn't mean we shouldn't proceed. It just meant we'd have to educate people, to show them what a functional family we had and demonstrate that our family, like any other, was built out of love.

For Susie, nothing had changed. She had made up her mind, and she was going to help her brothers. Drew and I decided we were ready as well. We were going to make a baby with Susie.

It was time to hitch up the wagon and head into uncharted territory.

THE CONFESSION JAR

JENNY FORRESTER

My mom said to me, "Do you have something to tell me?"

She held the jar I had not-so-thoughtfully hidden on top of the back of the toilet. We shared the bedroom and the bathroom, but she slept in the living room. We'd learned to navigate small spaces. She held the jar in front of her, like it was an ancient history-changing archaeological artifact—dangerous and precious and fragile.

She said, "Usually, when someone has a jar on the toilet, it means they're taking a urine sample for a pregnancy test."

I was trapped. I sunk to the floor and said, "Mom, I'm going to hell." Instead of the usual lambasting of my character, because I'd gained a couple of pounds (again) or because I neglected commas on a regular basis or because I wasn't a Midwesterner, she embraced me. We sat on the floor and cried.

Then, she rolled out a series of secrets that she told me to keep forever. She said that we were both hell bound.

I felt much better.

That moment was the beginning of confessions between us. We confessed in church on a weekly basis and confessed in our prayers, as often as needed. Confession wasn't new to us, but truth in confession—that was new.

I told her that I didn't use birth control because I didn't want to keep sinning, and that I never planned to sin, but it kept happening so I needed birth control.

She confessed to me that, at heart, she was a Democrat.

My mom, brother, and I lived in a trailer off the highway with a long driveway and a drafty barn where we hung the deer that we'd hunted. We attended a tiny white church with a few remaining stained glass windows, left over from the narrow-gauge train days.

We lived in an 800-soul town between Durango and Cortez. It was a churched town—Baptists, Methodists, Seventh-Day Adventists, Catholics, Jehovah's Witnesses, Episcopalians, and Mormons.

She said, "You can have kids without getting married."

And, "If you get pregnant, don't get married, because then you're making two mistakes instead of one."

She also talked about some girls in town, and said they had hinges on their heels. She said, "If you act like them, I'll disown you," and she said, "But I don't have to worry about you, because you're a good girl."

Mom raised me to beware of my reputation because it was all that a woman in a small town had.

So I took those mixed messages through the teen years and, just like my single mother, struggled through it.

There were reasons that we kept secrets and had a complicated relationship with morality and truth.

That town was one of those trucks-with-gun-racks-hunter-safety-taught-in-school-but-not-birth-control-options-everybody-believe-in-Jesus-in-some-incarnation-or-keep-their-mouths-shut kind of town. Mom's Midwestern roots, with that salt of the earth reputation to uphold and her status as a divorced woman when only women on the coastlines were doing it, threatened to create a bit of a tear in the social fabric.

All that was before the jar on the back of the toilet and before we started talking about reality in terms of actual events and feelings rather than through political or religious agendas.

I became adept at finding the right place and time for speaking difficult truths, but Mom struggled. She'd had more practice over the years at keeping secrets, creating an intricate web of life stories. Her confessions bubbled up and over.

She told me about old boyfriends, the ones I'd known—the rancher, the gun shop owner—and about others I hadn't known, the ones before my little brother and me.

We talked about painful things, too. She said that her long-term logger boyfriend, Vern, who took her two-stepping on Saturday nights, never took her to any of his Seventh-Day Adventist shindigs. He was ashamed of her.

One day, she said, "You know, I was pregnant with you before I got married."

I didn't know. We were shopping when she said this. I kept pushing shirts around on the rack, looking at them, looking at her.

She told me that I had been an accident, and that in those days, abortion was illegal. I said, "Think about how different your life would've been?" We talked about that for days and I never once took it personally, the way one might think.

I kept that jar beside my bed.

UNSPEAKABLE SACRIFICE

~~~~~~~~~

ANGIE MILLER

My mother lives down by the river. When you drive that way, you might see her clothes in black plastic garbage bags crammed under a park bench, or you might see her sitting, wrapped in a blanket, sipping a donated coffee from the local gas station. She's usually up early, before the sun rises, walking to keep warm. When the occasional tropical storm rips through New England, we try to get her up to higher ground, away from the danger of flash floods, but there's no guarantee she will move, since she usually thinks it's a conspiracy to remove her from her possessions.

My mother has mental illness. We think it's paranoid schizophrenia, because she hears voices from the FBI and an underground pornography/sex-trade ring. I say we think it's paranoid schizophrenia because we're not really sure, as we have yet to successfully get her involuntarily admitted into a psychiatric hospital to be fully evaluated and diagnosed. Don't get me wrong— we've tried. Multiple times. But they simply check her blood sugar levels, give her an eyesight test, make sure she's healthy, and then dismiss her while saying to me moments later, on the phone, "Your mother needs help." The police, the nurses, the homeless shelter—they've all told me this. "Your mother needs help." There's so much ambivalence and so little action taken to help her that I just want to scream.

Sometimes I see her in the grocery store. Her eyes get wide behind her glasses, like a deer in a comic strip, and her face becomes a mixture of familiarity, nervousness, yearning, and defensiveness. She just nods. I often pass her walking through our small town, her head down as she watches her every step, her brow furrowed into deep, permanent crevices, her mouth pursed into tiny lines of stress.

Despite all of this, when I talk about my mother's current state, I tend to do it in a joking manner. There's the time that she showed up at 3:30 in the morning and locked my dogs in the barn, and wandered into the woods behind our house, only to return four hours later, barefoot, in her pajamas, saying to the police, "I know this looks crazy, but I just wanted to pick some strawberries out back. Now, if you don't mind, I'm going to go inside and take a shower." Or the time she lost my childhood home, and when the new owners tore it down, she posted a sign in the front yard that said, "This house is still here. It is just underneath an invisibility cloak."

When I tell people my mother is homeless and crazy, sometimes I see blame in their eyes. How can I let my own mother live in the cold? How can I let her wander the streets all night long? How can I let her take free handouts of food at the local diner? What kind of a daughter would do this? What kind of a daughter am I?

Trust me—this is not the first time these questions have run through my head. Just this past Christmas, as my dad sat beside the fire with a big mug of hot cocoa and my children played games, their laughter filling every space in our home and my heart, I looked over at my husband, conversing with my brother-in-law, and my eyes grazed the table of food set out and I wondered what my mother was doing that night. My dad, as though he could read my mind, said, "I saw your mother today. Alone on Christmas." His eyes were sad, and he didn't really have to say anything else. I knew he was thinking back to all the Christmases we had once sat just like this—three of us kids with him and Mom, laughter, and food.

But guilt cannot dominate the complexity of my mother's situation. She has been kicked out of the homeless shelter, the senior center, the Meals for Many program at the church, my home, my grandmother's home, my sister's home, and my dad's home. Her mental illness has made her a threatening, aggressive, terribly mean person.

And so, a couple of years ago, after a particularly nasty encounter, I let the idea of who my mother was die. I let myself become an orphan. This woman was not my mother. This woman I pass on the streets, the one who forges my signature, who spends her days in the library keeping warm, who scares my children by telling them it is not safe to go outside—she is not my mother.

My mother had long, dark, lush hair and a quick, beautiful laugh. Having had me at seventeen, she raised me expecting more, and because of her, I was the first person to graduate from college in my family. My mother loved barbecues on warm summer nights and drank fruity wine coolers like they were soda. She made the most delicious homemade bread that she would let me cut into before it had cooled down. She read me stories at bedtime, attended my sports games, and came to every theater production I was in. My mother reprimanded me if I ever dared to judge anyone based on their appearance or beliefs, and she reminded me, through her own daily modeled perseverance, that it didn't matter that we were poor or that we were women— we were strong and wild and we would march forward and conquer our own fears and the barriers that others set down in front of us. My mother taught me to be courageous, empathetic, and grateful.

She taught me to work hard. She made unspeakable sacrifices for her family because she loved us, and she raised us to love our own children.

Which I do. The woman who was my mother—she would not want me to let the woman who is my mother now live with me. She would know that my life would be filled with anger, sadness, and danger. She would know that my children would suffer interminable scars, while living lifetimes of undying grief. My mother would want me to be a good mother, and a good mother is not one who allows strangers, which is what the woman I see now is, tear down everything we have built because we are filled with guilt.

My mother made unspeakable sacrifices for her family. She would expect me to do the same.

SHY

~~~~~~~~~~~~

HADDAYR COPLEY-WOODS

My youngest son is shy. Painfully, agonizingly shy. Picture day is a torment to him; raising his hand in class an impossibility. I once suggested he take a too-hot drink from the coffee shop into the subzero temperatures outside to cool it off, and rather than walk past all of those strange people's eyes to the door, he stubbornly scalded his tongue.

And this poor kid wound up with a mom who attracts stares everywhere we go. I am a disabled mom who has brain damage and a movement disorder, and I use crutches or a wheelchair to get around. I realized my son was noticing the stares the summer before he started kindergarten.

I sometimes do this thing I call the David Byrne—based on his trademark dance move in his "Once in a Lifetime" video: with no warning, I jerk my head backward with enough violence that the rest of me follows suit, staggering backward like a recoil.

We were at a museum, which is often the perfect recipe for this symptom; I was tired, overwhelmed, and surrounded by jostling people when I started to do the David Byrne like crazy.

I felt a chubby little hand steal into mine, pushing the crutch grip out of its way to grasp my fingers tightly, protectively. I looked down and saw my five-year-old boy glaring malevolently at a little girl of about three or four who was staring up at the twitching, flailing woman next to her, openmouthed.

Usually, when kids are staring, I stop and talk to them if they aren't too frightened. They have urgent questions about why a grown woman is behaving so strangely, or why she's in a stroller, or why she uses those sticks to walk. If their squirming, agonized parents will permit it, I happily answer their questions to help them understand and feel less fearful of disabled people.

This time, I ignored the little girl and knelt down eye to eye with my son.

"Are you upset that girl is staring at me?" I asked him.

He glared at her some more, holding my entire arm in a painfully tight grip.

"It is rude to stare," he said.

She ran off like a jackrabbit.

I explained to him that very young children who have never seen anything like me cannot help it; it is only rude when adults stare.

Several nearby adults jumped guiltily and moved to other sections of the museum.

My boy was shaking. Furious. Tears in his lashes. A five-year-old, feeling protective of his middle-aged mom.

I felt really shitty, of course. This is one of my worst fears as a disabled parent: that my kids will somehow be warped by my disability. Feel neglected or singled out or misunderstood, or become codependent. See their mom as a frail thing instead of the strong parental figure they need. Feel guilty when I get sick, or responsible for my well-being in a way other kids don't. I watched his angry tears on my behalf and thought: Well, I guess we all have to have *something* to tell our shrinks someday. We don't want them to get bored and nod off or anything.

But of course my humor was just covering up my sense that even when I'm not actively being a shitty mom, my body is forcing me to be.

Three years later, on a recent airplane trip during a flare-up, I am moving far more slowly than usual, and doing the David Byrne like crazy. I'm sure people are staring.

"Who am I?" my son asks loudly as he comes through security. "Who am I?"

He leans painfully on invisible crutches, jerking his head back at irregular intervals, his curly hair flying in all directions. I start to laugh.

"I'll race you!" he cries, and begins to run in slow motion, fighting desperately against unseen forces that slow him down as his head continues to yank backward.

Twitching and jerking, stumbling on real and imaginary crutches, the two of us make our way to the gate, roaring with laughter. I can hear, in our wake, the somewhat shocked and helpless giggles from the people who had been staring in pity. I can feel them smiling at us. He has completely turned the tables. I am in awe of him.

I have no idea how much it costs him, this extremely public display he uses to protect me as he did years before with his protective little hand and death glare—how much it costs him as an introvert, or how much it costs him as a kid.

I still worry that I am conditioning him to be more concerned with my feelings than a child should be. I think every disabled parent worries this: that somehow our disabilities will fuck our kids up. I worry that his clowning whenever he feels uncomfortable might make trouble for him later in school.

But mainly I take it for what it is: a tremendous, creative, beautiful gift from my son. You wanna stare? he says to the world. Fine. But you'll be staring on my terms.

And they are his terms.

And somehow, even as I worry, this moment, at least, feels right.

MOTHERING YOU, MY SON

In Six Chapters

~~~~~~~~~~~~~~~~

ANN BREIDENBACH

Chapter One: Yellow—for the sun that was shining on the day you were born, and the color of the outfit you wore home from the hospital. The year is 1982. I'm nineteen years old, a college sophomore, and single. My parents come to the hospital to pick me up. The social worker from the adoption agency comes to pick you up. You are going into foster care until I decide: Do I trust in the love of strangers and give you up for adoption? Or do I keep you, raise you on my own, be your mother? You're just a tiny bundle of yellow in the social worker's arms. I kiss you good-bye. And then I cry.

Chapter Two: Baby Boy Blue—the color of the outfit you wore in the photograph of you and me, taken by the Olan Mills photographer, paid for by my sister. I tried to keep you. For ten days. I brought you home to my parents. You slept in a white wicker bassinet beside my bed. My rosebud-covered journal sat on the bedside table, neglected—no time to write. I learned about diapers and bottles and baby baths and a mother's all-consuming love. I also learned about struggle and loneliness and the word "no." "No" was the word I heard when I asked for help. My own mother believed that a mother's love was grounded in saying "no" to her daughter. If I was going to be a mother, then I was going to do it on my own. It was the shortest ten days and the longest ten days.

Chapter Three: Gray—the color of the endless concrete highway that we traveled from my hometown back to the adoption agency. I only needed to make one phone call to the adoption agency to set things in motion. I asked if I could bring you back. That morning dawned cloudless and warm. We walked out of the house and piled into the car: my father, my mother, me, and you—my baby boy, Christopher, and all of your things. From the backseat, I stared straight ahead at the visible patch of passing gray highway, framed by my parents' heads. My father drove, silent in focus, tending to traffic, his palsied right hand bobbing up and down on the top of the steering wheel, manning the large Buick. My mother sat in the passenger seat, shoulders erect, staring straight ahead. I couldn't see her legs, but I knew they were crossed, elegantly, hands holding an unread newspaper, longing for a cigarette. You were tucked in your baby seat, next to me. That morning I had dressed you in my favorite outfit—the blue-and-white-striped onesie made out of the slightly silky fabric that made it special. No ordinary cotton onesie today.

Your long baby legs stuck upward, out of the car seat, feet snugly covered by white cotton sockies. You leaned slightly to the right, in the way that six-week-old babies do, in that posture of seeming resignation, shoulders slightly slumped. I carefully propped your head up with a flannel baby blanket, my hand lingering on your warm, round, silky head. Lulled by the steady hum of the moving car, you soon fell asleep. I wished I could fall asleep too, and dream beside you, but I was all too awake, living out this nightmare.

My father drove the familiar path to the adoption agency in Belden City. One hour total. Twenty-six minutes of flat farm fields. Twenty-three minutes of monotonous gray concrete expressway. Eleven minutes of shady tree-covered neighborhoods. Too quickly, we arrived.

Chapter Four: Beige—the color of the office file folders that contained the story of you and me, our family, authored by social workers. Ten weeks' worth of case notes. Ten weeks from birth to adoption. On that particular day the social worker wrote, "It is felt at this time that Ann needs to confront the reality of a permanent break in contact with Christopher." I went to court and signed the papers. Yours was a "closed" adoption—all secrets and confidentiality. I never even met the woman you would grow up calling Mommy.

Chapter Five: Black—the color of emptiness. Empty bassinet. Empty arms. Empty heart. Twenty-one years of the darkness found at the bottom of a deep, dank well. Black: the color of a "permanent break in contact."

Chapter Six: White—the color of the envelope that is delivered to my mailbox on the Monday following Mother's Day, 2003—twenty-one years after you were born. I don't recognize the sender's name, nor the address. I don't even know anyone who lives in Sault Ste. Marie, Michigan. Yet—in the flash of a light, the whitest light, I know who the letter is from. Knees buckle. Tears flow. With shaking hands I manage to open the envelope and take out the letter, unfold it, and begin to read.

Ann,

> *It's funny that I can write a research paper in a number of hours, but this letter has taken me nearly four years. It seems that I keep putting it together in my head, but never on paper. So here we go . . .*
>
> *In case you haven't looked and are rather confused, my name is Max. The last time we saw each other was 1982. You named me Christopher. . . . Anyway, this letter is just to say thanks, and let you know that I'm doing fine. You're an amazing woman. I understand why you did what you did. Thank you . . .*

Epilogue: Blue—for the blue of your eyes, the bluest of blues. And blue for the blue of your daughter's eyes, my one-year-old granddaughter, Emma. When I look into them now I see my own blue eyes, and it takes my breath away. "Say, 'Hi, Grandma Ann,'" you whisper to her. And she sings the sweetest "Hi . . ." and reaches her tiny arms out to me, fingers splayed as a baby's fingers do, offering love.

The End.

And the Beginning.

WHAT IF

~~~~~~~~~~~~~~~~

LISA PAGE ROSENBERG

Getting pregnant with our son had been a sweet shock. I had always wanted to be a mother but I was forty and had never been pregnant before. I came to accept the fact that it might never happen. Jeff and I had just celebrated two months as husband and wife when we found out the news.

Because of my age, mine was considered a high-risk pregnancy. We became regulars at the Center for Fetal Medicine and quickly became accustomed to medical tests and the three to five business days of anxiety following each one as we waited for results. I explained the process to Jeff's grandmother and told her I looked forward to the end of all the tests so I could stop worrying. "Oh, honey," she said. "I'm an eighty-nine-year-old mother. You never stop worrying."

As we got closer to our due date, the ultrasounds showed that our baby looked huge. My obstetrician was betting he might be in the ten-pound range. I imagined that all ten pounds of baby would be made of apple juice and Ritz crackers, the only things that helped me through three trimesters of nausea. My friends threw me a baby shower. The cat got used to sleeping in the crib we had set up in the room that would be the nursery. The months passed and I braced myself for the big event.

When I finally went into labor, I stood in our bathroom for an hour blow-drying my hair in my effort to control the uncontrollable. I may not have been ready for what was to come next, but my hair would be. Once we got to the hospital, we counted the time between contractions.

After fourteen hours, his large head and shoulders became stuck, delaying his entrance into the world, but he was delivered safely by cesarean section. Our nine-pound, two-ounce boy had arrived a week early. He was a big guy and he was perfect. We named him Bob, after Jeff's father.

My father was the youngest of eight and my mother was an only child. As a young couple, they pictured a future with a large family. When I was five years old, my twenty-five-year-old mother had some medical issues that could only be solved by a hysterectomy. My mom drove a green Chevy Impala station wagon, nicknamed the Green Dream, a vehicle large enough to carry the brood they were hoping to have. I bounced around alone in the back of that car for a decade, intermittently sharing the seats with Girl Scout troops and basketball team members. Like my parents, I had imagined myself with more than one child. I remembered the Green Dream as I drove the Sexy Beast, my old red Volvo station wagon with the single child's car seat in the back.

We tried for baby number two for a few years after Bob was born. When month after month it didn't happen, it became our usual twenty-eight-day setup for disappointment. Finally, we assumed that my limited biological window had slammed shut. I wanted to be grateful for the family we had, but I couldn't stop myself from missing the family I had imagined we could be.

By the time Bob was four and a half, my monthly cycle had become unpredictable. I chalked it up to perimenopause and waited for the raging hot flashes that would surely come next. One month I was feeling squishy and tired and lamenting my aging process. When my period was a few days late, I was not alarmed. Perhaps last month I'd already had my very last period. Then I thought, "What if . . . ?"

I came running into the kitchen waving the plastic pregnancy stick at Jeff. "Dude, I'm pregnant."

"Wait. What?" He turned to face me.

"Pregnant. I mean, right now."

"But that's what we wanted, isn't it?" Jeff steadied himself against the sink.

"That's what we wanted before, I guess we still want it. Right?"

"Right." We stared at each other.

"I think we're supposed to hug now."

Our shock carried on through the evening. We called our folks. "It's still really early," we told them.

We decided it was best to take it one day at a time and not to get too far ahead of ourselves in the planning. Meanwhile, we were already having conversations about where we might stow another person in our tiny two-bedroom house. We wondered how Bob would enjoy being a big brother. I worried about being in my sixties when he or she graduated from high school. If the baby was a girl, perhaps we'd name her Ruth, after Jeff's grandmother.

We got back in the groove of being at the doctor's office regularly. We had an early ultrasound that didn't show a heartbeat, but the blood work said I was still pregnant so we were told to keep a good thought and come back next week. I kept a good thought: a constant, worried, hopeful, good thought. I craved baked potatoes loaded with butter and sour cream.

Next we had an ultrasound that showed a weak heartbeat. We were told to be cautiously optimistic. I pulled out our favorite baby book, *The Big Red Barn*. We collected stories from friends who had "weak heartbeat" experiences with happy endings.

Back at the doctor's two weeks later, we found out the little heartbeat was stronger. We were ten weeks in and I was allowing myself to exhale a bit. I looked through the box of Bob's baby things to see what might be repurposed. Jeff sang "A Bushel and a Peck" and rubbed my tummy whenever he walked by. My new baked potato habit had reached unreasonable proportions. We settled in.

Bob reminded us daily that he would like a younger brother or sister and I was anxious to tell him the news, but we waited. I did not want to raise his hopes yet. Ours were raised high enough. "I love you a bushel and a peck, a bushel and a peck and a hug around the neck . . ." Jeff sang.

I noticed the first dull cramps as I picked Bob up from school. I was used to things shifting around during pregnancy, so I thought little of it. By late in the afternoon, I was bleeding. The cramps became more insistent. Something was wrong. Things had been going somewhat perfectly so far and now this wasn't perfect. I called Jeff and left a message on his work phone. I called my doctor's office and was placed on hold. I left messages for my mom and two of my girlfriends. I was in too much pain to drive myself to the doctor's office, and by the time Jeff called back, we wouldn't make it to her office before it closed. I put Bob in front of the TV and went into the bedroom. I silently prayed for the grace to handle whatever was happening and then, out loud, I took every swear word I knew and flung it at the pain.

At the emergency room, Jeff held my hand. We met a nurse and a doctor and another nurse and two ultrasound technicians. While stripping down to put on the thin cotton hospital gown, I noticed the chipped pink polish on my toes: one more imperfect thing. It was not a big deal and it was even less of a big deal right now but I needed to hide my feet. I slipped back into my red Converse sneakers and walked out of the changing room.

The ultrasound techs took too long with their tour of my insides. It was then I knew: We were losing this pregnancy. I stared at those red sneakers as the doctor looked over the test results. He wouldn't confirm what was happening. He did more tests and told us to go to my regular doctor in the morning to compare results. He did not want to give me anything for the pain. In the event that everything worked out, I shouldn't be on strong meds. It was a long night.

The next morning, my regular doctor confirmed that I had miscarried. I could expect to bleed and cramp for a few more days but the worst of the physical pain was behind me. Next would come the hard part.

My girlfriend Kimberly put it this way: She said, "We don't wait to start loving them until the 'safe' thirteen-week mark or the day they're born. We love them from the moment we walk into the drugstore to buy that test."

A few nights later, Jeff and I went out to dinner to our favorite sushi place. At the table next to us was a family with a little girl who looked to be about three. We quickly learned that her name was Mimi, as her parents did what they could to control her energy within the confines of their booth. Mimi's dark curls bounced as she ran between the tables, splashed in the koi fountain, played with her straw. Her father pulled her into his lap and she burst out singing.

"I love you a bushel and a peck, a bushel and a peck and a hug around the neck . . ."

Jeff and I held hands. We cried until the miso soup arrived.

SWIMSUIT EDITION

JENNIFER SUTTON

My daughter Sophie is five years old.

She has this pink bikini that she loves to wear. Her thin legs stick out the bottoms like a colt's and she has enough of that just-out-of-toddlerhood swayback remaining that her tummy sticks out, round and perfect.

She wears that bikini all the time, whether we're going swimming or not. She puts it on and dances around the house. She wants to wear it everywhere, to the grocery store or the movies or the park. That bathing suit makes her feel good. Complete. But for how long?

I think I remember at what age exactly I started to be self-conscious in a bathing suit. I was twelve years old and we had the end-of-school party at our house that year. I remember being so excited to have all the kids in the class to my house to swim in my pool.

I also remember wearing a T-shirt over my bathing suit.

Not coincidentally, that same year had marked the start of comments from boys in the class, comments about how skinny I was, how flat-chested I was, how they couldn't even tell if I was a girl or not. One boy, who could only be described as the most popular boy in the class, took to calling me the Young and the Breastless. And I would stand there, feeling my face flush as if it was on fire, and try to look at him like I didn't care.

Once I choked out, "That's not even funny. At least come up with something funny." And I turned around and walked off, aware of how my legs looked like toothpicks, how big my feet were, how the bra I was wearing kept riding up and needing to be pulled down. I'm quite sure now that the humiliation taught me something. But at the time, twelve years old and hidden in a bathroom stall not knowing whether to throw up or burst into tears, it felt like the end of the world.

How long will Sophie feel complete in her bikini? How long until someone makes some comment at the pool about those knobby knees or that sticking-out tummy and it occurs to her that she's not . . . perfect?

How long until that moment?

For now, I'll soak up every minute of her feeling free and strong and just right in that bikini. And when the time comes that some person says something to her that makes her feel less than that, I'll tell her this story: After months of that boy saying those things to me in sixth grade, I couldn't stand for it anymore. And on that day when he walked up and said, with a sneer in his voice and several friends standing behind him, "Hey, Jennifer?" I turned, always with that tiny, hidden hope in my heart that he would say something different to me, something kind or sweet. But he didn't. Instead, he pointed at me and said, "I've got a joke

that'll blow your tits off. . . . Oh, I see you've already heard it."
And his friends laughed. And he laughed, still with his finger
pointing right at my chest.

Well, I reached out and I grabbed that finger. I twisted it as
hard as I could, turning it and bending it with a strength that he
probably didn't imagine my puny little arms had in them.

I broke that boy's finger that day. And I wasn't even the least
bit sorry about it.

It was still a long while before I started to resemble anything
like a girl and, for years to come, I'd still put a T-shirt on over my
bathing suit. And I think about that still, these days with my
body nearing forty and having had three babies. And though I've
long since learned that none of us are perfect or ever will be,
there is always that moment. Every woman out there knows it:
that moment when you take off your shirt and your shorts at the
pool. It's that moment of self-consciousness, that moment of tugging down your bathing suit, sucking in your stomach, wishing
for the ten-thousandth time that stretch marks really are the
badges of honor that we like to say they are.

But I'm grounded quickly by looking over at Sophie, so con-
tent in her little bikini. She's waiting for me, waving at me to
hurry up and come to the water with her. She's watching me as I
adjust my bathing suit, pushing and pulling at it. She's watching
and, I realize, she's learning. She's looking to me for cues, for
lessons about how a girl is supposed to feel about her body, however it looks. She's going to mirror me and how I feel in my bathing suit.

So I stop. I stop tugging and pulling. I remember this is a
body that has grown three babies, nursed them all, rocked them

to sleep, carried them when they were tired, stayed up with them when they were sick or scared, walked them to their first day of kindergarten, hugged them, belly-laughed with them, and slept intertwined with them countless times. If I can't be proud of a body that's done all that, then what am I teaching Sophie?

And as I look at her, I see her knobby little knees, the ones she got from me. How can I doubt the perfectness of my own knobby knees now that I see them on her? I take her hand and we walk to the water together. Complete.

THE COOKIE JAR

~~~~~~~~

PATTY CHANG ANKER

I n 2002, after many years of wanting a child, my husband and I brought one-year-old Gigi home from an orphanage in central China. Our entire extended family poured love and affection, and yes, toys, all over her.

But she always wanted more. More toys, more food, more affection, in an at times frantic way. We knew from adoption preparation classes to look for hoarding behavior, but it wasn't that. She didn't stash food, she didn't steal from other people. But she was never satisfied.

When Gigi was four years old, we went to see the Christmas tree at Rockefeller Center. The crowds, the noise, the street vendors were overwhelming. Every two feet, Gigi pointed to another tchotchke, saying, "I need this!" I dragged her along until she planted herself in front of a man peddling Spider-Man toys, declaring: "I need more Spider-Man."

"No, you don't," I said. "You have plenty of Spider-Man. You have a Spider-Man bed, for crying out loud." Gigi paused, opened her mouth wide, and screamed: "IT'S NOT ENOOOOOOUGH!" All foot traffic on Fifth Avenue stopped.

We wondered if we were spoiling her. We lectured her about being happy with what you have, about how nice it is to share. Watching her struggle through playdates, it was clear that sharing did not make her feel happy, or nice. More like stressed and scared.

One night, after a kindergarten classmate had left with hard feelings, I sat on the edge of Gigi's bed to tuck her in and thought about what to say. Her large stuffed lion guarded her pillow.

"Imagine you have a cookie jar inside your heart," I began. Gigi perked up. She likes cookies. "Inside the jar are cookies that are made out of love. You act like you only have one or two cookies, and you're afraid that if you give any away, you won't have enough for yourself. But . . ." I was about to go on, about how love doesn't run out, how we can always make more.

But before I could, Gigi took in a sharp breath and cried. A deep, deep cry. "My cookie jar is broken," she sobbed. "There's only crumbs."

I held her and rocked her for a long, long time.

And then came Ruby. Were we ready for another baby? Gigi had been diagnosed with special needs. The house revolved around her. Meanwhile, in Wuhan, China, Ruby was the center of attention in her foster family. Only child plus only child? How was that going to go?

It went . . . loudly. It was *Crouching Tiger, Hidden Dragon* meets the WWF. I wanted to give them capes and fighting names. Ruby may have been five years younger, but she had the build of

Roseanne Barr, and like Roseanne, what she lacked in speed she made up for in vocal power.

Once Ruby learned to grab and run, every night went like this:

Gigi: "That's mine!"

Scuffle. Thud. Ruby dropping to the floor, *scream scream scream.*

Gigi: "I'm telling Mooom!"

One night, as I was prepping dinner and praying they would parallel play until I could get it on the grill, my husband came in from the yard. "C'mere," he said.

"I have to skewer these kebabs before the kids lose it," I said.

"It'll only take a second." He steered me out the back door and pointed at the sky: pink and orange. Beautiful. He put his arm around me. Before kids, we hiked mountains for views like this, for quiet like this. How long had it been since we'd looked at a sunset? I smiled at him. He leaned to kiss me, and—

"I'm telling Mom!" Boom! Out flew Gigi, skidding to a stop next to us.

"Heeeey. Whatcha doin'?" She was suspicious. Mom and Dad don't usually stand around doing nothing,

"We were having a moment," Daddy said.

Gigi looked us over. Then a lightbulb went on. "Oh, I get it," she said, snuggling her way between us. "Were you guys thinking about . . . back when . . . it was just the three of us?"

In Gigi's mind, those were the good old days.

But in those days, Gigi didn't know anyone who needed as much as she did, who yearned for love in the same bottomless way. She didn't have anyone who could show her exactly how to comfort and be comforted.

But when Ruby was three and cried, "Nobody loves me," Gigi could see, objectively, it was not true. "I love you," Gigi said. "Mommy and Daddy love you." When Ruby, at four, cried, "What if Mommy stops being my mommy?" Gigi replied, with certainty: "Mommy will never stop. Forever Mom is forever. That's her job." Reassuring her sister, herself already reassured.

The other day, Gigi, now ten years old, asked, "Can we organize my room? I've got a lot of stuff I don't need." I could hardly believe my eyes, as she dove in, scaling mountains of toys, sorting the truly cherished from the rest. Letting things go.

"I don't need this Spider-Man anymore," Gigi said, putting it in a stack for Ruby. "I have plenty."

I smiled. The cookie jar is full.

MY MOTHER THE PROTECTOR

~~~~~~~~~~~~

EDDY JORDAN

I saw my mother die 2,601 days ago and I have thought about it every day since. Not to keep a record going or to prove a point, it just happens that way, it's inevitable. When a woman like that enters your life for even a minute, the rest of the world is just a waiting place until she comes back to you.

She was the woman who battled three separate diagnoses of breast cancer, who worked three jobs to help her three children. She was an avid watcher of soap operas, who would call me over to her lap and catch me up on the episodes I missed, since I only watched Cliff-Hanger Fridays. She was a determined woman, adamant and persistent, and on many occasions would find any excuse to debate my father, my favorite of which was her bold contention that the correct song lyric was not "cat scratch fever," but actually "cat scratched the beaver." She was deeply invested in her children and believed wholeheartedly in their talents. She bore the burdens of the world with a beautiful smile and she was Xena the Warrior and the omnipresent Band-Aid applicator extraordinaire. She was the hulking protector.

It's summer and Mom is inches away from my face. There is a

shockingly cold plop on my nose and I wince, but then I man up because big boys don't wince when their mom puts sunscreen on their nose. She sculpts my face and I relish the bubblegum scent that she bought at my request. My skinny feet are tap-dancing from either the heat of the patio concrete or my poorly restrained excitement. I know that this is the last step before we load up the car, because it's a sacred formula. On field trip days I watch her prepare the lunches, helping where I can. My big projects are typically spoon-licking endeavors, which Mom tells me I have a particular talent for.

All of the day-care kids arrive, and my mother manages to collect us into the van. You don't think of the word "patience" when you think of a carload of children, but my mother had developed superhuman tolerance over the years. We finally reach the crest of a hill and catch a small glimpse of the destination: Elitch Gardens, but the cool kids called it Six Flags, so naturally I called it Six Flags.

I don't remember much of the other rides we went on that day, but I'll never forget the teacups. My buckle was hard to get out of on the previous ride so I'm the last one off, which means I don't get to pick my partner in the teacup. This leaves me face-to-face with my sister on one side and me on the other and a large mysterious plate in the middle. I'm not a fan of being very dizzy, so I let my sister Amy know I don't want to spin a lot. She looks at me and laughs. "Eddy, you can't control the ride—if you don't want to get dizzy, you should get off."

My sister is two years older than me, so I don't question her. I unlatch the little door on the teacup and step out onto the platform. The second my foot touches the platform, the ride starts moving. I'm not at my academic peak at this point in time but I still know that this is not good. I'm bobbing and weaving between the teacups that are currently moderately fast but are rapidly gaining speed. Of course, my natural instinct is to run over to my mother, who is a couple teacups and a black iron fence away.

With my third-grade athletic abilities I manage to jump three quarters of the fence, which is awfully similar to jumping zero quarters of the fence. I fall into a crevice in between the platform and the fence, where my back is on the fence and I am facing the rotating platform. A gear catches my shirt and my back is being dragged across the fence. Meanwhile the ride operator couldn't be more oblivious, though I do think she was beginning to suspect something by the heart-wrenching shrieks issuing from my mother. But this woman still hasn't pieced it together.

I have gone one full revolution and I am offered front-row seats to the most humbling image I have ever seen. My mom is raising hell, moving through the crowd like they're not even there. She reaches the control panel and lunges with all her supernatural strength at the operator. So my mom is at some foreign control panel looking directly at me and decisively slams down a fist on a large red button. And I am saved.

This is the kind of person my mother is. Once someone plows into a ride operator to save you, you're indebted to them. That's just a basic unwritten rule. But in January of 2006, she was diagnosed with breast cancer for the third time in her life. It wore on her and wore on her until the doctor informed us the cancer had metastasized into her spinal fluid, and at that point all you can do is wait for it to take you. So I watched this woman, whom I loved more than I was capable of loving anyone or anything else, slowly and inevitably die.

She couldn't speak in her last week, but she managed to tell us all one last thing. She passed away on April 1, 2006, April Fool's Day, as if to say, in her kindhearted, light-spirited way, "Fooled ya. Although you might not comprehend it now, this is not the end."

There are not enough lifetimes that I could repay my debt of gratitude to my mom. How do you repay someone to whom you owe everything?

COCKTAIL PLAYDATE DROPOUT

~~~~~~~~~~~~

STEFANIE WILDER-TAYLOR

It's four in the afternoon and I'm at a playdate with all three of my kids at the home of a "fun mom" from my older daughter's class. A couple of her friends and their kids are here trying to burn off the long march from afternoon until bedtime known by parents as "the witching hour." When the inevitable chilled bottles of white wine come out, they're met by audible groans of relief. But when the glasses are handed out, I pass with a smile and a simple "Not today, thanks," like I'm just not in the mood. I'm a mom who doesn't drink anymore.

One of the moms who doesn't know I'm in recovery glances at me funny sipping on my Diet Coke. Which I totally get. Two years ago a couple of kids, a bottle of wine, and with any luck a few Vicodin left over from someone's C-section sounded like the perfect playdate, and I had no trouble finding other mothers who shared my enthusiasm for better parenting through chardonnay.

Drinking worked for me. It worked to lessen the anxiety, the fear, and yes the boredom that I felt as a mother. It also helped me bond with other parents who still thankfully enjoyed an adult pastime like wine. Maybe the other mom is worried I'm judging her. Maybe she thinks I'm sipping my soda and wondering, "What kind of mom ties one on with her kids underfoot?" But of course that's not the case. The truth is I miss it.

I miss how alcohol allowed me to tolerate conversations about breast-feeding, the horrors of public school, the importance of organics, and the few other topics my life had narrowed down to. For me, drinking helped to bridge the gap and allowed me to feel a part of rather than apart. I authored two books with alcohol-infused titles: *Sippy Cups Are Not for Chardonnay* and *Naptime Is the New Happy Hour,* and sang the praises of the cocktail playdate. I even went on the *Today* show twice defending the practice of drinking with other parents as a perfectly acceptable social practice.

And when there was backlash on the *Today* show website or the Amazon reviews of my book, I felt defensive. After all, I wasn't telling people to down a bottle of wine, smoke a joint, and maybe swig a few shots of their kid's prescription cough medicine to get through a day at the park. I was suggesting the ancient notion that drinking in moderation can ease the pain. And that's how I believed I drank. Until I didn't.

By the time my daughter was two I was questioning myself and wondering if I wasn't becoming dependent. I was a daily drinker by then, often grabbing a glass of wine with lunch if I could. But then I got pregnant and didn't drink through my whole high-risk pregnancy. Eight months and not a drink. Problem solved. Nothing to worry about here, folks, clearly I can stop anytime.

My consumption picked up ahead of where it left off with the stress of having preemie twins. It morphed into daily drinking combined with Xanax and a feeling that after a glass or three I didn't want to stop until I was completely out of it. I drank all evening, every evening, and found that even if I tried, I couldn't take a night off. But I didn't cross any lines. Instead I moved them back inch by inch.

Although I always drank in a way I now know is abnormal, it was still easy for me to believe I wasn't an alcoholic. Alcoholics are homeless gutter drunks or slurry, abusive moms swilling mouthwash when they run out of Bushmills. I was simply a woman who had a little too much wine at night by myself or with my husband while my kids were asleep and out of harm's way. I was definitely not an alcoholic. I was so much better than that. Until I wasn't.

At the last cocktail playdate I attended before I quit drinking, apricot martinis were the order of the evening. I found myself swilling a few while a nanny stood by watching the children. Finally, after a long day spent worrying about my one twin with failure to thrive, and playing cruise director for my four-year-old, it now was my time. The buzz took over, my off switch disengaged, and I had quite a few before I finally strapped my kids in and drove home, most certainly over the legal limit.

No matter how far back I'd pushed the line, I'd just gone crashing over it. For the first time my husband was enraged at my drinking, and for the first time I saw myself as clear as day—a mess who just barely avoided becoming Lifetime movie fodder. I had just played Russian roulette with everyone I love.

A few days later I attended my first twelve-step meeting and I've been sober for almost two years. So now the truth is I feel out of place at the cocktail playdates I used to find so amusing. So when I feel the pull and I want just one glass so I don't feel so different, I remember that I am different. At least when it comes to how I drink. I've driven drunk. I've gotten so drunk I've puked repeatedly on a first date. I've done things I don't remember, and don't care to remember. I've embarrassed myself and other people. Worst of all, I've let myself down as a mother. To stay sober today, I can't let myself paint a prettier picture of my problem.

But the benefits of no longer being a drunk mom are plentiful. I take more pleasure in parenting; instead of rushing through the small moments in the evening to get to "my time," I've finally realized that it's all my time. My marriage is much better since I stopped picking fights with my husband, and when we do argue, at least I remember what I was mad about in the morning. I have a new appreciation for my mom friends who never drank much in the first place. Plus I've acquired sober mom friends with whom I'll discuss everything from recipes to *Real Housewives*. But not scrapbooking. You have to draw the line somewhere.

THE MOTHER OF ALL FATHERS

ROBERT SHAFFRON

have a husband, two children, and a membership in the PTA. At home, I do the majority of the cooking and the bulk of the laundry, arrange most of the playdates, e-mail the teachers, assist with the school play, sign the homework, enroll them for camp, and comfort the guinea pig. Moreover, I have been known, on numerous occasions, to utter the phrases "Actions have consequences," "If it goes into the laundry inside out, it goes back in your drawer inside out," "Am I speaking a foreign language?" and even the timeworn but ever reliable "If you learned your multiplication tables the way you learned those damned song lyrics . . ."

What I mean to say here is, despite all appearances to the contrary, I'm a mom. And since currently I'm self-employed (a cunning little euphemism for unemployed), I'm now a stay-at-home mom.

Some years ago, back in the halcyon days when we had a nanny to spend all day with the boys and schlep them all over the place, I took my son Benjamin to a little evening concert that was being held at the school. As we entered the building, one of the maintenance people saw Ben and said, "I know you! I see you with your mother all the time!" A bit ruffled, I puffed up a tad, looked her in the eye, and said, "No. I'm his mother."

And while I'm here, can I just set a little something straight, so to speak? I've heard repeatedly from some, um, factions, that having two parents of the same sex confuses the children. I'd just like to confirm, in no uncertain terms, that my children are not confused about having two dads. They are frequently confused about racism, long division, cruelty to animals, deodorant, war, lima beans, and typewriters. But they are crystal clear about their family composition, and have never even thought to question it. We're all they've ever known. And, because we live in a very progressive and diverse (read: normal) community, none of their friends, neighbors, or teachers are confused either.

In fact, at Ben's third birthday party, a little girl who was there had a tear-fueled, full-tilt breakdown upon learning that Ben had two fathers. When asked by a panicked gaggle of concerned grown-ups what she was crying about, she blubbered, "I want two daddies, too!" Not confused. Just disadvantaged.

One more thing my children seemed sort of confused about was why their parents weren't married. A few years back, when Jordan was six, his voice floated up from the backseat of the car—the site of most truly consequential discussions. "Are you and Daddy going to get married?" (By the way, my husband is Daddy, and I'm Papi, which is a whole lot less sexy in real life than it sounds.) In response to our son's question, I glanced into the rearview mirror and launched into a fulsome diatribe, detailing the inequality of New Jersey marriage laws, the oafishness of our tone-deaf governor, the disparity between our state and the more enlightened states, and the general injustice of the connu-bial system in our nation.

When I paused to breathe, Jordan interjected, "Well, if you get married, are you gonna dance?" It began to seem as though perhaps I had overanswered. I considered his query for a moment, and replied, "Yes. Yes, I think we will dance if we get married."

He caught my glance in the rearview mirror, narrowed his eyes a bit, and said, "The tango?" Clearly, the boy has his priori-ties in order. Not confused at all.

As it turned out, New Jersey did the right thing, and now, after twenty-seven years, we are married men. Our sons were the ring bearers at our wedding ceremony. Just as they were the ring bearers when we became domestic partners. And just as they were the ring bearers for our civil union.

So when our kids bitch about their parents, they have the same exact repertoire of complaints that all the other kids have, no matter what gender combo they have at home.

And while I suppose technically speaking my boys don't have to listen to their mom per se, they're not actually getting away with anything. Because when I have to, I can be a real mother.

A MUCH-NEEDED SLAP
IN THE FACE

~~~~~~~~~~

YOON PARK

I grew up in a typical immigrant family. I was born in Seoul, South Korea, and my family and I moved to the States when I was three years old. Because I was so young when we emigrated, picking up a new language and culture was a nonissue for me. And as in many immigrant families, my parents relied heavily on my older brother and me, for that very reason, to help them interpret and navigate this country.

And as a typical kid, I was self-absorbed. I was cocky. I was highly inconvenienced whenever my parents would ask me to translate their bills or doctor's orders or whatever needed clarification.

One day when I was in college, learning about socially and politically marginalized groups, finding my own voice, and exercising my leftist activist leanings, my mom asked me to look over something for her. I don't recall what it was, maybe a bank statement. No matter, I was dismissive as I usually was. With little attempt, I'm sure, at hiding my frustration and impatience, I tersely translated what was on the page, not checking for or caring for actual comprehension.

Sweet mercy, I fumed, my parents had been in the United States for nearly twenty years, and they still couldn't understand a simple document? It was embarrassing. It was worrisome. It made them look bad. It made me look bad. And most of all, it made it glaringly clear that we didn't belong.

My mother's voice interrupted my darkly clouded thoughts.

Actually, her silence did.

She turned and looked at me, or maybe she didn't. I must reiterate how consumed I was by my own pride. I was too busy resenting the situation to really pay attention to anything or anyone else.

But something had changed in the room, something that made me present. I remember my mom said very matter-of-factly, "I am not stupid."

There it was. My mother had finally voiced what I would never admit to feeling. Her tone wasn't angry or sad. Perhaps there was a hint of irritation, but really it was a calm affirmation of her worth. And it was a much-needed slap in the face for me.

With surgical precision, concise and accurate in execution, she put me in my place. Or rather, she assumed her rightful place as the incredibly strong and capable woman she is, deserving my utmost respect. She didn't have to say anything more. I was left alone to confront . . . myself.

And I was ugly.

I was so caught up in trying to gloss over my family's roots that I adopted the very thing I resented: I had adopted that oppressive, racist view of the world, of my parents. I cringed at kimchi, broken English, and slanted eyes. As those were the things I feared would define me, I had started defining my own mother by them.

And here she was, calling out her supposedly enlightened, college-educated daughter. I had to face it: I did think my mother was . . . lesser. Somehow I had equated her not being fluent in English to her not being intelligent, her needing my help to her being weak. My mom, who worked seventy hours a week and simply did not have the luxury of time to perfect her English. My mom, who learned not only to survive, but thrive, and nurture her family in a new country. My mom, who made the best kimchi-*chigae*, didn't need to speak a common language to communicate warmth, and was the most beautiful woman I could ever know. I thought she was lesser.

I was such an asshole.

And yet, she is my mom, my *omma*. She is quick to laugh and quick to forgive and forget. So a few years later, when I had matured enough to own what happened that day, I mentioned it to her. I told my *omma* how it was the very slap in the face that I needed to jar me out of my ignorance and arrogance. She laughed and asked incredulously, "Really?" (*Jeen-jah?*). She claimed she did not remember this incident, and then she apologized to me for making me feel bad! "No-no-no!" I cried. "It was what I needed! I'm thanking you!" I told her. I don't think she quite understood what I was trying to say. We still have our translation glitches.

Our mothers are usually our first and most important teachers. We expect that they will teach us basic survival tips, personal hygiene, cooking, reading, and the like. We know they are full of wisdom and love, giving us what we need when we need it.

I needed a slap in the face that day, and I got it. My mother taught me that I had it all wrong. For all the times she told me I was beautiful, it was when she allowed me to see myself clearly that I could move forward and stop embarrassing my mother.

IDIOPATHIC

～～～～～～

AMY WILSON

Your son is fascinating," the doctor said. "I mean, you hate to tell a parent that, but it's true."

We're standing in a sort of double-doored hallway, an air lock, like something on a spaceship. I can see my seven-year-old son looking at me through the window. He's tethered to his hospital bed by a tangle of wires coming out of the top of his head, cabled together and running to a machine on a pole.

He's been in that bed for two and a half days.

I wave back at him, smile, like I'm just standing on the other side of the fence at baseball practice.

"I wish I had some answers for you," the doctor says.

I just look at her. That was the whole point of my coming out in the hall to speak privately. That was the whole point of our being in this hospital at all: this moment of truth, good or bad, that would make it all worthwhile.

"Look, we've ruled out a lot of bad things," she says. "You should take comfort in that."

She is right, of course. There are kids in this hospital far sicker than mine. There are parents who stand in this hallway and get heartbreaking, world-ending news. But this is my child.

"We're calling it idiopathic," the doctor says, "which means we don't know why this is happening. Maybe it's called that because all the doctors are idiots. Who can say?"

She chuckles a bit. My son is leaning forward on the bed now, trying to see me through the window. He knows we are talking about him. And even though I do my best to hide my distress from my child, the look on my face cannot help but tell him what all these hallway conferences have been about: There is something wrong with him. And nobody can figure out what it is.

The first time my son fainted, he was on a field trip with his first-grade class. The gods were kind: I was standing right behind him when it happened, and the field trip was to a fire engine museum. The avuncular and CPR-trained firefighter serving as docent took his pulse, sat him up, and got him some orange juice.

Kids faint, his pediatrician said that afternoon. And yes, now that she mentioned it, it had been a little hot in there. But two weeks later, I found my son unconscious on the floor at home. When he finally came around, his lips had no color at all. Let's run a few tests, his pediatrician said. Just to rule things out.

Later that week I watched with a detached interest as the neurologist attached electrodes to my child's skull. My son and I chatted the whole time about the conquest energy levels of various Pokémon. I could be breezily reassuring because that was how I felt. My husband hadn't even come along with us. Why skip an afternoon of work for one just-to-be-sure test? And so it was only my child and me sitting there with the neurologist twenty minutes later, when he told me my child had not been fainting at all: he had been having seizures. I could feel my son's eyes on me, trying to calculate my reaction to the doctor's big words. I parked him in the waiting room with an old *Highlights* magazine and made it to the ladies' room before I cried.

My son started medication that night. He kept fainting. He changed medication. He kept fainting. That's when we met the "idiopathic" doctor, who took him off all medication. He stopped fainting. For a year. Then it started again with renewed purpose, and it has continued that way, on and off, for two years since.

And after four more hospital stays, after five other medications, after nine more doctors, after MRIs and tilt-table tests and EEGs and EKGs, there are things we know: It's not his heart. It's not his blood pressure. It's not his blood sugar. It's not cataplexy. It's not his nervous system. It's not his fractionated catecholamines. There are things we choose to be certain about: It's not in his head. It's not in my head. And while some events in his now dishearteningly thick patient file might have been seizures, most were probably not. And so we are left with two possibilities: to keep searching for an answer, or to accept that we might never find one diagnosis that can explain what this is and how to make him better.

Maybe a better mother would have more acceptance. Maybe a better mother could live in the most-of-the-time that her child is just fine. When I do stand on the other side of the fence at baseball practice—where my son has never fainted, or collapsed, or been anything but happy and running and nine—I feel sure that for his sake we should embrace the uncertainty, say no to even one more test. But then the next day while he is at school, my cell phone will buzz in my pocket. "He's fine," the school nurse will say. "He's here, he's fine." And then: "It happened again."

My worry for my idiopathic child is there at all times, just beneath the surface, a lump in my throat that will not go away. How do I calibrate my concern when I have no idea what I'm concerned about? And how do I reassure everyone else who cares about him when I have no explanation to provide?

That is why, standing in that hallway with that doctor two years ago, I wanted a diagnosis. I wanted something I could wrap my head around, make a plan, take a sample, engrave on a bracelet. And there are still many moments where any answer at all feels better than none. But there are other moments when I fear that the message my child is getting from all of this testing, from seeing the worry on his mother's face, may be more dangerous than whatever is wrong with him. And so perhaps "idiopathic" is the best diagnosis, after all.

I looked up that word's etymology last week. (I admit it: I needed something to research, and I'd already Googled everything else.) "Idiopathic," the dictionary told me, comes from the Greek, for "private suffering." And therein I found my answer: even if worrying about a child is a mother's job, I cannot let my desire for clarity come at the cost of my son's childhood. If my child is ever to be truly healthy, he must be free from fear—and my fear, above all. I cannot let the things I don't know become more important than the things I do: My son is idiopathic. And he's "fascinating." And he's mine.

NICK'S STORY

~~~~~~~~~~~

NADINE C. WARNER

veryone thinks their firstborn is special.

But Nick really is.

We got him when he was a week old after a year and a half of bureaucratic bullshit. When we started the process, we're like, no-brainer:

Find an agency.

Pay your money.

Get your kid.

Done.

International was out, 'cause, you know, a lesbian couple adopting from China? Yeah, like that'll happen. So we go domestic.

Our agency is all sunshine and light and *pro-black* with the kente cloth everywhere and our social worker, Julie, is a walking stereotype—white liberal Mama Cass lesbian with three black special needs kids. She *assures* us that they do "a lot of same-sex placement."

But what she should really say is this: "Here's the deal. No one's going to pick you. Birth moms are all like, 'I ain't want my chile wid one of dem gays.' So, you're getting the leftovers—the ones that people have returned or simply left at the hospital."

Julie has us put together "The Book," which is this weird five-page *marketing* piece that says, "Hey, Birth Mom, we've got money, a lot of it, and live in a really nice but unidentified part of the city. We're an interracial couple, surrounded by black people, so your kid will feel right at home. Pick us. Oh and yeah, we're gay but we're *friendly* gays; we're chicks who look like chicks."

We do all of this work on the book and Nick's birth mother never read it. But this other birth mother did.

Let's call her *Makeda*. Eighteen years old, one kid already, second kid on the way. She's two hours late to our first meeting and our enthusiasm has waned by the time she shows, but she hooks us with *"I really want you to have this baby."*

And it's all smiles after that . . .

Till Julie calls us the next week to tell us that Makeda's in a bit of a financial bind right now, and so often in cases like this, the birth mothers simply disappear.

We shell out three grand, find her a place to live because, according to Julie, her home life is very stressful, and it's not good for the baby. Then a month later we're taking her to her doctor's appointments, because now public transportation is not good for the baby.

In the end, she decides to keep the baby.

And Lori and I are, like, "God, this is never going to happen." In the room we thought would be a nursery by now, we spend the whole night praying—that intense, head's gonna explode, body-rocking praying. "Just please, please, just give us a baby."

A few days pass before Julie calls us at work to tell us they have a baby boy, born with the cord around his neck and six fingers on each hand.

The cord around his neck could mean anything from a temporary air restriction to serious brain damage. I tell Julie we want a pre-placement screening, but she snaps that there are plenty of families who will take him without one.

So I snap right back that I don't care.

Then she finally relents and says she can meet us at the doctor at 2:00 p.m.—at his house because he's on vacation.

And we're so jaded by this point, we're like, hit McDonald's, skip the car seat. We stand outside this beautiful rehabbed Victorian for ten minutes before someone finally answers the door. And it's this crazy white-haired aging hippie who smells like patchouli and sounds a little high. *This* is our doctor and he's a little *dirty*, like the whole house is a little *dirty*. He's got two overweight Labs lounging on the sofa . . . licking themselves.

Then in walks Julie with this bundle. She makes a beeline for me, 'cause I've got "sucker" stamped on my forehead, and she places him in my arms.

He's so *tiny*. At seven days old "Baby M" is pruney and pale, with thick straight hair that's matted to his forehead.

In the background I hear that he's got a heart murmur, to check those extra fingers for bone, that we've got no tox screen . . .

And we have a choice. We can give him back to the social worker until all of his test results are in, or we can take him home and just see.

So then Julie chimes in that he can go back into interim care, but it's not going to be the kind of nurturing environment he needs.

Shut up, you stupid cow.

Lori looks down at Baby M and cups his head in her palm. Then I look into his eyes . . . and that's when I know. I just know.

We're taking him home.

Aw crap, we don't have a car seat.

Julie jumps up from her seat and races for the front door. She's got one in the car.

After we strap Nick in, I rattle off a list of items we have to pick up at Target as Lori babbles about rescheduling client meetings, inviting family over, sending out birth announcements . . .

Then we remember to breathe, to savor the moment we became parents, though it feels as if he has always been ours. I look back at Nick, and a blissful silence descends upon us as our twenty-first-century alt-American family settles into being.

I turn to Lori. "Hey, Mommy."

She smiles. "Hey, Momma."

We have the perfect son. He's just extraordinary.

He's our Nicholas.

PREPARE TO BE JUDGED.
AND POSSIBLY STABBED.

JENNY LAWSON

Becoming a parent subjects you to a whirlwind of new and strange emotions and can leave you feeling more vulnerable than you have ever been in your life. It is at this exact moment that you will find yourself set upon by strangers intent on telling you exactly how terrible you are as a parent. You might think that you'll easily brush these criticisms off, as you are now a grown-up who understands that you are master of your own destiny and that peer pressure is something you overcame in high school, but then you'll find yourself in tears because someone said your child will be a drug addict because you got an epidural, or that you should be forcibly sterilized because you put your kid on a leash.

That last one there? Not a joke. Totally happened to me. I was walking to the park with my daughter and she was wearing her halter and a woman rolled her eyes in disgust and whispered, "Some people shouldn't be allowed to have children," to her friend. Then I turned to her and said, "SOME PEOPLE have children who have a hereditary condition that makes their elbows prone to dislocation at the slightest tug and if they hold their child's hand and the kid falls then their elbows get dislocated and then SOME PEOPLE have to take their child to the doctor to watch the doctor put their tiny, screaming child's elbow back in the socket. Maybe *SOME PEOPLE* SHOULD MIND THEIR OWN DAMN BUSINESS AND STOP BEING SO FUCKING JUDG-MENTAL OR I WILL STAB SOME PEOPLE IN THE FACE WITH MY KNITTING NEEDLES."

That's exactly what I said. Hours later. In my own head. I would never have said that out loud. Mostly because I don't even *own* knitting needles. And also because I was still so unsure of my parenting decisions that I couldn't defend them out loud. Which is sad because I was a *great* parent. And I still am. Not per-fect. Not flawless. Not faultless. But great. And unless your chil-dren are currently locked in the bathroom while you go on a two-day bender, I suspect you are, too.

As long as you are a parent you will be judged and will be given unwanted advice. There will always be someone there to criticize you, but the good thing is that there is also someone there to criticize *them*. It's a vicious cycle of blame and guilt and the best way to remove yourself from it is to realize that what-ever decision you make for your family is the right one for you.

The circle of shame as overheard at a park:

"I can't believe that you drank Coke during pregnancy. *I* only drank warm milk. Your baby will probably have ADD."

"You drank *store-bought milk*? That's loaded with antibiotics and steroids. Your baby is like a tiny Incredible Hulk. *I* only drank milk from my own personal cow."

"You drank raw milk *during a mad cow epidemic?* How terribly irresponsible. I drank only purified bottled water from artesian wells."

"*Bottled* water? Fabulous. So you're the reason why my child will inherit a world filled with overflowing trash dumps. Way to shit on Mother Nature, asshole. *I* drank tap water from one reusable cup. I even brought it with me to the hospital during labor."

"You had your baby in a hospital? How cold and meaningless for you. I had my baby at home, and my other children helped with the birth and then my husband cooked the placenta for us to eat."

"So you forced your family to become cannibals. How wonderful for them. *We* planted our placenta with a sapling in the park to celebrate life."

"*You disposed of medical waste in the park. OUR PARK? Are you fucking kidding me?* My kid is playing under a placenta tree? You don't *keep* the placenta. You throw it away."

"You *threw away* your placenta?! WHAT DID I JUST SAY ABOUT THE OVERFLOWING LANDFILLS? Why aren't you composting? It's like you're *TRYING* to destroy the earth."

"Well, maybe I am. Maybe me and *my Hulk baby* are trying to destroy the world *using only store-bought milk and my placenta.*"

"Oh, my God, you are *totally* overreacting. I blame all that store-bought milk in your system."

"YOU WOULDN'T LIKE ME WHEN I'M ANGRY."

"Oh, is that a TV reference? We don't own a TV. It's not good for children."

"*Children?* With current overpopulation issues you still decided to have children? We have limited resources and your decision is just plain selfish. I'm keeping my IUD, *thankyouverymuch.*"

"YOUR IUD IS MAKING THE BABY JESUS CRY."

"YOUR ANTIQUATED RELIGIOUS VIEWS ARE TEACH-ING MY CHILDREN INTOLERANCE."

"YOUR CANNIBAL BABY JUST BIT MY BABY BECAUSE YOU TAUGHT IT TO HAVE A TASTE FOR HUMAN BLOOD."

"TERRY, DON'T BITE THE HULK BABY. IT'S FULL OF STEROIDS AND RAGE."

"I WILL KILL EVERYONE."

And that's why I don't go on mommy-and-me playdates any-more.

MONKEY, SPEAK

ROBYN RASBERRY

My daughter, Bela, dropped the F-bomb for the first time when she was four years old.

She was on the floor playing with a pride of plastic lions. The baby lion had wandered away from the mama and daddy lions, up the treacherous slopes of a cereal box mountain. The baby lion was trapped under a clear plastic cup. The mama lion, spotting her cub first, rushed up to the plastic prison, searching for a way to rescue her baby. After a moment, the mama lion yelled through the plastic in desperate frustration, "I'm sorry. I can't get you the fuck out of there."

It was this opportunity I took to explain to Bela that some people might find what she just said offensive, but she didn't get in trouble. I always tell my daughter that, when she is with me, she is allowed to use any words that she wants. No word is off-limits. At school and/or Grampa's house, however, things are different. In these places, there will be consequences. There will be trouble. There will be punishment. But not when she's with me.

I'm a linguist by hobby and a lover of all things language. I try to teach my daughter that words are simply sounds that come from our mouths. The sounds are oftentimes less significant than the sentiment behind them. I tell Bela, "It's not always what you say, but often how you say it." So, as long as she is exercising respect, she's allowed to use whatever words she wants. And she does.

As a six-year-old, she now repeats words she hears from the grown-ups around her. "Pissed off," she'll repeat quietly, cutting her eyes toward me with a giggle. "Hell, yes; shit, no; oh, my God; damn it." She likes to play with the boundaries of the sounds that roll off her tongue, and I enjoy watching her try them on.

I enjoy watching her form a thought and articulate that thought carefully. "Mama, I feel like I need a day to rest," or "I'm curious about why the sun is so bright." Some of my favorites are "Do you know what a symbiotic relationship is?" and "Why don't you eat your own boogers?"

She blows my mind on a daily basis. It's fascinating to hear even a fraction of all the ideas cooking and swirling in that brain of hers. I love to hear all of it. I don't ever want her to experience a wall between her thoughts and the vehicle that brings them to communicative fruition.

I'll be honest, though; this approach is sometimes less than awesome. I have my less than favorite sentences that have surfaced. "What happened to your hair?" or "Why are you so grumpy sometimes, Mama?" or "I'm not as pretty as my friend Emma."

Recently, Bela asked to speak seriously for a minute. She said, "I have something to say, but it will hurt your feelings, Mama."

I said, "Monkey, you are always allowed to tell me what's on your mind."

With sad eyes, she looked away from me as she spoke. "I like living with Daddy better. I am more comfortable at his house." I did everything I could to hold back tears and gently asked her why she felt that way. "Well," she said, "at Daddy's I have my own room. And he has his. And there are comfortable clothes to wear and a clear table to eat at and do my homework."

This particular comment rendered me heartbroken.

A couple of years ago, my dad let me move into his tiny, 900-square-foot home after my divorce. He helped me in no small way to get back on my feet and to start building a new foundation for Bela and myself. We were squeezed into a small space for longer than we would've liked, but we made it work.

I can see the reasoning behind the sacrifice, but Bela only saw us sharing a tiny room and that I couldn't afford to buy her new clothes when her legs magically grew two inches overnight.

Her confession made me think of all the times I threw nonsense at my mother. "Why are you always so tired?" "Why can't you be like other moms?" "I'd rather live with my dad than you." I think about how that must have made her feel. Single mom, working the night shift at the hospital, putting herself through RN school, begging my brother and me to eat our vegetables and get to school on time.

I've never really asked her about it, mostly because of how ashamed I am of my bratty behavior, but I imagine my mom questioned her decisions every day. "Should I quit school? Should I be more present? Am I failing at motherhood?" I imagine these questions became louder in her head when I would go off on my verbal tantrums. But I can say with confidence now that she did me a service by making those sacrifices. She improved her own life and, in turn, taught me to do the same. I am self-reliant, determined, driven, and capable because I learned from a strong woman how to be.

I want to do the same for my daughter, so I constantly ask myself, "How do I raise my kid the right way? How do I do it right?" We all make little decisions, even unpopular ones, hoping to do it right. We sacrifice our minutes with our children and go to school to improve our living situation. We encourage our kids to articulate their thoughts, even if those thoughts are painful for us. We examine our own shortcomings in the most vulnerable ways in order to help our kids avoid the same pitfalls we experienced.

Encouraging Bela to exercise freedom in her speech and communication is one of my ways of trying to do it right. Because when it's all said and done, Bela has to grow up and go out into the big, bad world. Just like I did. Just like my mom did. I want to know that Bela can enter the world as a woman and be able to wield her communicative powers to capture the things most important to her. I want her to be able to say without hesitation, "No, I don't want to sleep with you, even if that means you won't like me anymore." "Yes, I'd like to accept the position if a comparable benefits package can be arranged." "No, Officer, I didn't steal this duck." Or, "Mom, I need your help."

All of the choices we make as mothers are in an effort to help our children avoid those moments in life from which they cannot escape. Above all, I'm trying to prepare Bela to hold her own when she gets herself into an impossible situation, because she will. We all do. I want her to have the ability to survive if she ever gets cornered or trapped, especially when all I can do is turn to her and say, "I'm sorry, Monkey. I can't get you the fuck out of there."

THE WONDERING

~~~~~~~~~~~~~~

GRETA FUNK

was making dinner the other night, and my oldest son, who's almost seven, was sitting on the floor on the other side of the island, reading a book. Without looking up, he turned his attention to me. "Mama, can you tell me again how my dad died?"

I've told him and his five-year-old sister about their dad many times in the last couple of years. Not going into too much detail, but showing pictures and making sure that they know who he was and what he was like.

"Sure, bud," I say as I cut up the cauliflower for roasting.

"He was driving home one night when a lady that should not have been driving hit his car and killed him."

I've never gone into many more details than that, unless one of my two oldest asks me a specific question.

"Were you wondering where he was?"

OOF. The knife stopped midair as I sucked in my breath and felt my heart start to race.

I didn't want to say, as I tried to catch my breath, that yes, I was wondering where he was. I didn't say that I called his cell phone fifteen times in the span of an hour because I knew he should have been out of his class by then, one of the few classes left in his college career. That I, his barely pregnant wife (so early in my first trimester that we were the only two that knew, save for our obstetrician), was driving home from my own class, on my way to pick up my then-one-year-old son. That I made a couple of extra calls to my parents, who were babysitting, to find out if they had heard from my husband. That I must have left a dozen messages on his phone and that it was possible that the paramedics, who were probably cutting him out of the car at that very moment, heard the phone ring.

And ring, and ring.

I didn't tell him that they must have left the phone in the car as they loaded my husband, his father, into an ambulance and took him to the nearest hospital, only to load him into a helicopter because his injuries were too severe and he was losing too much blood. I didn't tell him that it wasn't until I got home, and saw the blinking light on the answering machine on that winter night nearly six years ago, that I began to realize that something was very, very wrong, or that I searched for words when the 911 operator told me that my husband had been in an accident and she would try to find out exactly where he was, but that inside I was losing control and my mind was racing in a thousand different directions.

Or that I could barely speak as I called my mom to tell her that something had happened, and no, I didn't really know what, but they're telling me that his legs are crushed and he's in the hospital and can you please come over right away?

No, I didn't say that the other night to my nearly seven-year-old son when he asked me the innocent question that literally took my breath away.

"Yeah, buddy. I tried to call him and didn't know where he was until I talked to the police."

I took a long, deep breath and continued to chop, knowing that as they get older, the questions would only get harder to answer. And wishing there was a manual for this sort of thing.

But there isn't, so I find myself writing my own. Not knowing how to do it, or what to say, just like I didn't when I listened to that answering machine message, and like I didn't when I got to the hospital with my mom late that night and waited outside the emergency room for hours before hearing any news, then practically living in the surgical ICU for four long days before he was declared dead. Just like I didn't when I delivered our daughter seven months later, surrounded by friends and family and intentionally festive luau decorations but without him, my newborn's daddy. But I did it, I somehow did it. And I'll somehow do this: answer their questions.

Because while my children lost their father, they didn't lose me. And I am their mother. While I watch them grow, help them learn, and try my best to make them understand, they are helping me write the chapters of the manual that I so desperately wish I had.

BE HAPPY, HAVE A GOOD LIFE, REMEMBER ME

ANN STEWART ZACHWIEJA

M y daughter was born in China. She has a birth mother. She has me. And she has another mother, too.

We received our daughters in a hotel conference room in Guangdong Province in the year 2000. These shell-shocked little babies had ridden on a bus for hours, to be transferred into our arms after a quick diaper change. They were too young to understand what was happening, unable to voice their confusion beyond desperate cries or catatonic stares. From time to time they craned their little necks to look over our shoulders at the orphanage personnel who had brought them to us—reaching out with tiny hands toward the women standing around the room's perimeter.

And here's what I was thinking. You have a *mother* now. Look at *me*, little girl. I'm your *mama*.

Beyond the theoretical, I hadn't thought too much about the "Aunties," the women who had cared for our daughter during her first year of life. I was wrapped up in preparing for a long trip to China and wondering how I could leave my five-year-old son behind while I went halfway around the world. I knew they were important. I knew they had a hard job. And I knew they had kept her safe and alive until we could come and get her. They were the means to my end, and in all honesty, I hadn't thought about what it might feel like for them.

They were the women who had loaded our little babies onto the bus in the morning and gone back to their day's work with the remaining children.

We were fortunate enough to visit the orphanage the day after we met our babies, being the first-ever foreigners allowed inside. Upon our arrival at the Lianjiang Social Welfare Institute, we were ushered into a conference room, offered tea and the local fruit called "dragon's eyes." As we sat around a large table, listening to speeches of goodwill and nation-to-nation commitment, a swarm of Chinese Aunties suddenly swooped into the room and scooped up the babies whom they had, just the day before, released to their new lives. I can just picture these women anxiously waiting outside the doors—desperate to see the little girls they had held, fed, changed, washed, sung to. It's not hard to imagine that longing, that ache in their arms.

Of course, one of those women was there for our daughter. She rushed to our baby, picked her up, and cried and cried as she held her close. She firmly patted her face, her hair, her arms—as if to reassure herself that this precious child had returned. What was she thinking when she realized who we were? Was she relieved? Was she sad? Did she want her back? What was she thinking?

Our shared baby happily settled into her Auntie's arms, quiet and clearly relieved to be back in the place she knew, with its familiar sights, sounds, and smells around her. Their eyes met as she drank her bottle of rice cereal and formula, her Auntie's tears dropping onto her little face. Their bond was evident and tangible. Here was this gentle woman, fiercely holding our daughter and nuzzling her face in the last short time they had. What must that feel like? Was it harder since she'd probably already done it once, as she packed her into the bus that would take her away?

Through my meager grasp of the Chinese language and the use of universal gestures, we asked this special woman to write our daughter a message on a piece of hotel stationery. At first she didn't want to, but we persisted. As she sat writing and crying, my husband videotaped this intimate moment. Can you imagine anyone taping you while you write a letter to a child you love, knowing it will very likely be your very last communication? How can one say all that is in her heart when given so little time and such a small piece of paper?

> *Wode hao nuer,*
> *Zhong Guo mama zhu xing fu kuai le he nide xin*
> *mama, baba. Kuai kuai le le kuai gao zhang da.*
> *Zhong Guo Mama*

> *My dear Daughter,*
> *Your Chinese mama wishes you happiness with your*
> *new mama and daddy. I know you will have a good life.*
> *Your Chinese Mama*

So you see, my daughter has me, and she has her birth mother, and she has another mother, too—her Chinese Auntie, who loved her with all the intensity of a mother's love.

I sometimes go back and look at pictures from that day. There we are in the conference room. There is our daughter in her Auntie's arms. There we are outside as a smiling group, our daughter's beloved Auntie standing right next to us. I'd know that face anywhere, and I've seen it since in pictures from other families who have adopted from this same orphanage.

How many children has she sent into the world? To how many children has she whispered these words?

Be happy. Have a good life. Remember me.

MY MOM FOUGHT THE NAZIS AND WON

~~~~~~~~

BRIAN LAVENDEL

When the German army marched through Warsaw, Poland, in September of 1939, my mother was eight years old. A daughter of two middle-class Jews who identified more as Polish than Jewish.

My grandfather, Lolick, was called into the Polish military. He and others fought in the mistaken hope that if they held the German army off long enough, England and France would come to their aid. He was captured by the Soviets and it would be seven years before my mom and grandmother would see him again.

In Warsaw, the Nazis took control of daily life. Some relatives used international connections and money, made their way to Switzerland or Palestine, and then New York. But my great-grandmother was ill. Too sick to travel. My grandmother refused to leave her. And my mom refused to leave her mom. It wasn't long before they did not have the option to leave. They were confined to the Jewish Ghetto.

With help, my mom and grandmother found hiding outside of the ghetto. My great-aunt's husband, Uncle Franek, was a

Yugoslavian diplomat and a non-Jew. He arranged false papers for my mom, a new name, and she was taken in by a Catholic family. She recounted that while living with her new family, she once wrote her real name over and over again on a piece of paper so she would never forget it, then tore the paper to pieces and flushed it down the toilet.

I still have a photo my mother carried with her while she was in hiding. It's a blurry image of a female figure in the distance wearing a hooded winter coat. It turns out it was my grandmother in the photo; Franek gave my mom permission to carry the photo of her mom only because one couldn't clearly identify who was pictured there. But my mom knew whose photo it was, and that was all that mattered to her.

About halfway through the war, having survived three years in hiding, my mother watched the Jewish Ghetto of Warsaw go up in smoke. The Nazis systematically burned and blew up the buildings as they sought to crush a small but persistent holdout of Jews who were determined to fight back. Between previous deportations to the death camps and the burning and razing of the ghetto, three hundred thousand Jews died. My mother would later say she felt guilty for not being among those who perished.

In the end, seven years later, after the war was over, my mom, my grandmother, and my grandfather reunited. Crushed and wounded but not beaten, they made their way to England. Their hoped-for destination, the United States, had strict immigration restrictions on the numbers of Jews admitted. My mother ended up at a British boarding school, where she said she "understood English but didn't speak it."

After boarding school, she started medical school in Dublin.

There she met her first husband and gave birth to a daughter, my half sister, Yvonne. But being a young parent didn't prevent her from earning her medical degree in psychiatry as one of only a handful of women in her class.

From there, she and my sister made their way to New York City to join my grandparents, who by then had received permission for the family to immigrate to the United States.

My mom died in 2008. For a time, I was angry and bitter. I was choked with selfish questions. Then the questions I pondered began to change. I wondered: What was it like for her? What must it have been like? Coming to this new place, having been exiled from her home with barely her life? There were so many untold stories.

But before she died, my mother gave me a gift I treasure still. She and I traveled together to Warsaw. We stayed in an old house, one of the few that remained from before the war, since so much of the city had been pounded into rubble. She once again walked the streets of her hometown, now so different from when she was a child.

We were walking arm in arm down one of the main avenues in Warsaw, traffic passing and people bustling on the sidewalk, when my mom stopped for a moment, seeming to focus on something far-off. "There was a broken water pipe here," she said to me.

You see, in August of 1944, nearly five years after the Germans first invaded and took over the city of Warsaw, the Polish underground resistance held the German army from parts of the city for two long months. My mom was a courier for the Polish underground. They would move through the sewer pipes to deliver messages or supplies, avoiding and outwitting the Nazis wherever they could. On one occasion, my mom was passed over for a particularly risky mission; the job was given instead to a girl who was a bit older. My mom would later watch her die from the injuries she sustained in the course of the mission when parts of a burning building collapsed onto the girl.

This street corner, I learned, was where they came to get drinking water during the uprising. It was also where she greeted Uncle Franek for the last time; he was killed in the first few days of the uprising. My mother was thirteen years old.

During our visit to Warsaw, I would catch my mom gazing out of our apartment window. She was mesmerized by a small run-down vegetable stand across the street. I realized it probably looked much like it might have sixty years earlier. When we stepped into that cramped stall to buy green beans or radishes, I watched her take delight in selecting a few vegetables and in speaking her rusty Polish with the grocer, who was so kindly toward her. I imagine it was like a return to some nearly forgotten other world for her.

She told me that when she was a new immigrant to the United States, no one asked her about her life history, not even her therapist. No one could listen to the horrors she lived through.

As for the unanswered questions, I suppose I will always have some. Many years ago, I interviewed my mom, asking her about her life before, during, and after the war. We were sitting under the palm trees beside the pool at her home in Florida. We took a break from the questions. It was one of those clear, comfortable Florida days. She glanced up at the fluttering palms and peaceful blue sky surrounding her, with a look of wonder across her face.

She let go a sigh, made a sweeping gesture with her arm, and then, as much to herself as to me, said, "I never imagined I would end up in a place like this." It is only now that I am beginning to understand what she meant.

Recently, my wife and daughter and I traveled to Warsaw. We walked those same streets, this time without my mom. I pointed out to my daughter where her grandmother came for drinking water during the war. We met with the woman whose mom hid my mother during the war. Her granddaughter translated for us. And so my nine-year-old daughter got to hear tales about her grandmother from someone who knew her, remembered her, grew up with her, who lived with her in her hometown. We rode an open-air tourist bus around the city. We walked through the old town, reconstructed to look as it had before the war. We stopped at memorials honoring the heroes of the uprising. "Your *babcia* was one of those," I told my daughter. The sky was blue and the Wisla River was shining. And I felt as if I were experiencing the gift of watching one of life's great circles coming around to complete itself.

I WANT TO BE A NOTHING

~~~~~~~~~

JENIFER JOY MADDEN

My mom looked like a *movie star*, resplendent in zip-up sweater, turtleneck, and tastefully dangling earrings. She sat patiently as I clipped on the microphone. I was making a video to celebrate her and Dad's sixtieth wedding anniversary.

As I centered her in the viewfinder, I wondered how she always managed to look just right. Her hair—short and chic. Her clothes—stylish but not showy.

When I was little and she went to a dance with my dad, she'd sweep down the stairs and I'd feel like a gray mouse cowering at the skirts of Cinderella. She looked perfect: two parts Audrey Hepburn, one part Lucille Ball, with gowns sleek and sparkly enough to make my Barbies jealous.

When I was about five, I remember twirling around the house in my pink tutu. Dad was at work and my brother didn't bother much with me, but Mom was my constant companion. I had my own word for what she was: a "Nothing"—and that's what I'd say I wanted to be when I grew up.

After all, she was always at home, wearing at-home clothes.

She had no job title. Since I could think of nothing to call her, I declared that's what she was. And she never corrected me.

Over the years, my attitude changed. When I graduated from college, I was off to the Big City: *Washington, D.C.,* where I'd won a federal internship. The guy I had dated since I asked him out senior year soon followed—and not long after, we were married.

When he got into medical school, I jumped from government to media, climbing the news ladder up from obscure satellite channel to the Big Leagues at ABC.

Along the way, we had our first child—a daughter—and I vowed she'd *never* aspire to be a *Nothing.* I even bought her clothes in the infant boy's department because I'd be darned if she was typecast in girly pink and purple.

With memories swirling, I pressed the record button and asked Mom about life before Dad. She looked off a moment, then addressed the camera.

"I finished high school and was working at the telephone company where my dad was a lineman. But I couldn't stand being an operator. One day, I read about a contest to get into college, so I took that test and *won*—a four-year scholarship. I was in the first class to graduate from D'Youville College of Nursing."

Hmmm, I thought. I knew she went to college when her family couldn't afford it, but I didn't realize she was a *Self-Made Woman.*

She went on. "I met your father when I was a student nurse and he was a student doctor, after he noticed me in the cafeteria line. One day, as I was taking care of a little boy, he came up behind me and said, 'Do you always give your charges this much attention?' Well, I looked at this forward medical student, then I turned on my heel and left him crib-side!"

When my dad asked around about the pretty brunette, a jealous friend fibbed that Mom was engaged, so he tried to forget about her. But Mom didn't forget him, as she told the camera:

"I needed a date for the graduation dance. My *mother* actually found his number. So I called—and asked him to go."

Had I heard that correctly? My mom asked my father out *first*? But that's what *I* did! I thought *I* was the assertive one.

Still expecting to portray her as a homebound product of the '50s, I asked what she did after the children arrived.

"Well, if you consider your father was in practice forty years, I worked about half the time—answering phones, taking blood, weighing patients."

That's right, I thought. She *did* work part-time. I didn't much notice because she was always there when I got out of school. Things were sounding uncomfortably familiar. After my second child, I became a freelancer to spend more time at home.

Finally, I asked what she thought were the happiest days of their marriage, knowing full well it had to be when they were *graced* with my brother and me. "Our happiest?" she asked with a faraway look. "Well, I'd have to say it was right after the war when Dad and I were stationed in the Philippines."

What? I almost blurted out loud. Wasn't that *before we were born*? Here I was, fifty years old, and still thought I was the Best Thing That Ever Happened to Mom.

Then it hit me. With no book to tell her the color of *her* parachute, my mom had masterfully blazed her own trail—and *I* was no more mold-shattering trendsetter than she was relic of the past.

As I switched off the camera, I felt *incredibly lucky* to have her as my role model and I realized: My mom was never a *Nothing*. Oh, no. She was, and still is, *Really Something*.

MOTHER

A Multiplication Lesson

~~~~~~~~~~~~~~~

DANA MAYA

am thinking about a math problem I have been living for many
years. The problem is simply this:

How many is mother?

What is it to multiply, to be a body-within-a-body, a strange
kind of two?

And then they say there is a division, the birth as a severing, a
return to the "one" you were before. But mothers know that there
is no such return. In this multiplication-and-division problem,
there is always a remainder. Something resists solution, falls outside. Birth is not the end of a multiplied self but its very beginning.
Despite this, a strange and faulty math persists all around us,
attempting to parse out in clean numbers what will not subtract
and can never divide. In the talk of postpartum bodies, you may
hear the phrase "She got her body back." These words are like dull
gossips, too blind with desire and fear to notice that this ain't no
weekly weigh-in, sweetheart. A human emerged whole from the
body of another human, you see. The lesson is this: That mother

body won't be "gotten back." Her body exceeds the confines of what "body" meant before; she has ramified, sent out tendrils, flowered.

Because mothering is a difficult math problem, though, there is not only *more* in the sum, but also *less*. So many parts of our lives: gone. We lose what we need (sleep), what we crave (choice, solitude). We lose relationships and vanities, routines and sanity. And we see, as the losses slough off of us, slow, then fast, what is now as plain as our own skin: there are a great many losses to come. When we flower, then we see.

How many is mother, then?

Is it the sum of the number of children you raise, plus yourself? Is a partner added in? How many are you? At times, mother is a many-headed beast, a tiny crowd of arms, legs, breasts, feet, mouths, sweat, milk and blood, chromosomes and space. At other moments, it is lonelier than solitude. A mother knows the loneliness of the guard: at attention, alert, unable to lose herself to sleep or to dreams. A mother is unable to wander.

In my own multiplication lesson, I had to understand that I had two babies—twins—inside me. How *many* is "twins"? How many is the baby-I-had-imagined-in-me times *two*? I've learned that the answer is not easy: the answer is both more and less than *two*. There were two amniotic sacs, two placentas, but only one uterus, one big pregnancy. Was it one birth or two? Am I a different mother to each of them? How many are we three?

And then, I am ashamed to admit, it took me some time to realize that their father was part of the calculation, that he changed the math in surprising ways. I realized, late, that it would not be me, *one*, torn between *two*, but it would actually be he and

I, each of a pair. And even better, the partners could rotate in a kind of a square dance: first, he and I, and the two babies together; then this baby with me, that baby with him, and then we'd "swing 'round and switch." This describes how we live now, four people as one organism, splitting off and recombining. Sometimes it's a graceful dance. Other times, we break and splinter. There are tears, regrets, and careful stitches later.

When I used to meet a mother of one baby, she and I would look at each other and try to understand the difference with that faulty math. Bewildered, she'd say, *"I can't imagine."* She'd think, "What I know, times *two*?"

And I'd try to reckon how what I knew split. But twins are not another baby multiplied by two. Twice the effort, twice the work. They're not "double-trouble!" as the grandpas called out on the street when I walked by pushing my twin stroller. They are twice the breast milk, two bodies, two minds, two diapers to change (at once). But they are also one spoon in one big bowl, one bath, one tall pile of clothes, a life, side by side.

They defy the numbers *one* and *two*. I look at these small twin people, my children, and I think, *They have always been together, from the very beginning.* But count again and it's true for each of us. Each of us is born of a mother, born of another. Every one of us: multiple.

Of all the identities I have lived, mother is the one that has most multiplied me. I am Mexican-American, a child of immigration, a Coloradan, a feminist, a writer. In living the worlds that pass through me, I have lived inequity, aspiration, mental illness, margins, and belonging. More than any other experience, though, it's mothering that has opened me out—out—further, and then further, to multiple allegiance, so that I feel more than ever before that *I am like her,* and *them.* And *her* too, and even, god, yes, *her.* I stand in the checkout with her, I hold the door for them, I notice her tears on the airplane. She is poorer than I, she is richer than I, she is from a culture like my people, or she is not. I can see her mother experience all over her, though. I see it without wanting to. I feel her close to me, and I cannot shut my heart to her.

First, mothering multiplied us, out—into the small bodies of our children. We satisfied their hunger before our own. It was not grandiose; it simply was. And then we kept multiplying, not into more children, but into more lives. I could feel other children, other caretakers, and the children that lived contained within the adult bodies in my midst. The small constellation of my own family was evoked by every other family constellation moving around me.

And all the mothers out there: Are we one mother or many? The answer, of course, is yes.

We are mothers, multiplied.

ALL YOU NEED IS LOVEY

~~~~~~~~~~

KATIE WISE

What I've found most absurd about motherhood are the things I will do to keep my children happy.

"We can't find Orange Shirt." These five simple words sent me into a panic when I received this text message from my son's day care.

I texted back: "I'm on it, bringing backup." I dashed out of work, as quickly as one can dash eight months pregnant, into the volcanic July heat. Speeding toward my sister's house halfway to Denver, I looked at the clock. I had forty-five minutes. Only forty-five minutes until that special time of day, which mothers all over the world both treasure and dread. Nap time. Without Orange Shirt, there would be no napping.

Orange Shirt is my three-year-old son's lovey. A lovey (binkie, wubbie, num-num) is a transitional object, transitioning the child from their mother's love to self-soothing skills. Our ancient monkey reflexes make us fall asleep easier if we hold on to something (i.e., a mother, an iPhone, a tree branch, or an orange shirt.)

My nephew's lovey was known as Stinky Ducky because he sucked on it until it reeked like bleach, mold, and cat pee put together. I'm still stunned that he held it so close to his face without vomiting. After my husband met Stinky Ducky, he was over loveys. He hadn't used a lovey, and he determined our children (not even born yet) would not need loveys. I failed to tell him about my own history with loveys: my good dream pillow that I loved from age three—now a shred in a box in my mother's garage—and my soft down pillow from college, called Softest Softest, which is still on our bed today.

There is no stopping those who want a lovey. At four months old, my son attached himself to my orange maternity tank top that said "expecting baby" on it. And it was lovey at first sight. He called it "dootch" when he couldn't say "shirt," and now it was called Orange Shirt.

When he was two, we cut it in half. The "expecting baby" half was home Orange Shirt and the other half was traveling Orange Shirt. When traveling Orange Shirt had been left at my sister's the night before, home Orange Shirt, in a rare moment, left the house, and went to day care with my son, where they had (carelessly, I might add) lost it. We had gone from two orange shirts to none in less than twenty-four hours. A missed nap would not be good, but if we didn't have an orange shirt by nightfall, I shuddered to think what would happen.

I arrived at my sister's at thirty minutes before nap time. She said she had left Orange Shirt in the barbecue grill outside her house, before her early morning plane flight. I confidently lifted the lid, and saw only black wire racks and old coals. I felt like I was in a reality show, designed to make pregnant women freak out like hyenas on camera.

I checked every window and door that a pregnant woman

could safely reach. I looked under every rock, plant, rug, welcome mat, all the likely places for a hide-a-key. Even though I knew they were on a plane, I called my sister and mom. Don't you know this is an emergency? I screamed to their cheerful outgoing messages.

Luckily, there was still Bob. My stepdad Bob was the one you call when your computer isn't working, or you're locked out of your house, or your hemorrhoids have gotten so bad that you can no longer drive (which was me a month after this story). I called Bob's home and cell, but he had forwarded his two phones to each other, rendering them both useless. I looked again for hidden cameras.

Nap time was approaching faster than a whore on roller skates.

I called my sister's neighbor, Kathryn. I called her eight times and finally got through. I tried not to cry, but you know when you've been trying to call everyone else in the world and they are all abandoning you like your dad did when you were three, and every guy you dated till you met your husband, and you finally reach someone who is alive and has an ear, and you're eight months pregnant and it's 108 degrees outside and you're in a desperate hunt for a half an orange tank top that will probably save your child's life?

I cried. A lot. To this day this woman probably thinks I'm a total lunatic. Calmly, she talked me through how to find the key to my sister's house. Inside, in a plastic baggie next to the door, forgotten in a rush and looking like trash waiting to be taken outside, was the slightly less-preferred version of my son's lovey. I grabbed it and got back in the car.

I drove to my son's school and burst through the gate like Mercury. My son had skipped nap entirely, but strangely seemed fine, playing outside in the sandbox, confused to see his mommy's red, tear-streaked face. Then his teacher said, "I think we know where the other one is."

She explained the morning's adventures, while my mind raced. How could they let him take Orange Shirt to a park? Would you take the *Mona Lisa* to a day at the beach? I suppressed my rage and disbelief through a pursed-lip grimace. I thought of reporting them to social services, but I couldn't waste the time. Orange Shirt was out there . . . somewhere.

Now I really was on reality TV. I waddled out of the gate and heaved my sweaty mass of pregnant self into the car.

I pulled up to the nearby park as a homeless man was walking away with a small red wagon full of stuff. For one crazed moment, I imagined he had definitely stolen my son's lovey. Why wouldn't he? It's very soft.

Trying to remain calm, I rolled down the window and said, "Excuse me?" I wasn't going to be this close and fail. "Excuse me, sir. Did you happen to see half of an orange tank top?" I was trying to be cool, but my red eyes and shaky voice betrayed me. He stared at me blankly for a moment and then said, "Yeah, I think it's in the gazebo."

Cue *Chariots of Fire* theme music. I ran across the park, my big belly bouncing. Looking like an old pair of underwear, abandoned on the cement, was Orange Shirt. I held it to my face, inhaling that sweet stinky-lovey smell—familiar and warm.

I felt for a moment what my son must feel when he holds Orange Shirt. Like it was all going to be okay. Like this crazy shred of fabric, worn by me with my son in my belly, and loved by him every night, was a soft fabric umbilical cord of love between us, connected once again, never to be broken.

Someday I'm sure he will lose something I cannot retrieve for him, his innocence, his first love. But that crazy July day, I had caught his fall. I saved his lovey, that symbol of my love, to take with him out into the world. The world might eventually fail him, but not his mother.

THE UPSIDE TO DOWN

~~~~~~~~~~~~

MERY SMITH

The upside to Down is when you think you've fallen, you've really just begun.

The upside to Down is the understanding that you've joined a whole new club. One that is cooler and better than you could have ever imagined.

The upside to Down is smaller ears, smaller hands, and smaller eyelids. Smaller everything. And isn't everything, including shoes, cuter smaller?

Hobbs is my youngest son. Born just 449 days ago. He is what the textbooks call developmentally delayed. Special. Some older references would even say "retarded." It's not okay but I don't think they meant it the way it feels. Hobbs came with the magic number, trisomy 21, and that means he has Down syndrome.

Somewhere, deep down, I guess I knew that this would happen. I declined the genetic testing offered with both of my pregnancies. I was afraid of what I might do if I did know, like for sure know. Would I judge him? Would I for a moment not love him? Put this diagnosis in a box and label it "bad news." It was better for me not to go there, so we didn't.

You just know some things as a mom. Sometimes, we can predict the future and the fate of our children. Before they fall backward or grab the wrong thing off the table we're there for them, easing their pain and avoiding the mess. But with Hobbs still inside me, I couldn't do any of that yet.

He was evicted on a short-term lease contract at thirty-seven weeks. I remember with my first son, Otto, who also came via cesarean, the sense of relief I felt when the doctor brought him out, despite the whole numbed-from-the-waist-down thing. With Hobbs's birth there was no sign of relief. They pulled and yanked and sewed and stitched. I cried and cried and cried holding hands with a stranger. A nurse who, after Hobbs was born, asked me, "Why are you still crying? He's here. It's over."

It was far from over. Have you ever been in a room full of machines, and teams of people, and a newborn baby, and a husband, and a mom and heard nothing? Silence. That's when you worry. Go ahead and freak out at that point because something is definitely wrong. It was belief that had me spinning; there still wasn't any proof.

Until there was.

Our doctor very gently began to describe Hobbs's physical attributes: the fold over his cute little ears, the one crease in the palm of his right hand, the beating in his heart. It looked and sounded like Down syndrome. It felt as though someone turned off the oxygen in the room. Everything I thought I knew about God, myself, our family, everything was in limbo.

There is a crossroad in grief. A point in which you can turn into fear, what-ifs and why-me's. I tried that path momentarily. Would he ever go to school? Have a job? Go to prom? Get married? Live with me FOREVER? I mourned the loss of certain dreams I as mother had for Hobbs. Then I realized those things aren't necessarily promised to any of us. We're all living one day at a time. We don't get to know our life story. Not on day one or fifty years from now.

"What do we do?" These simple words fell out of my mouth. A nurse, no saint, looked me straight in the eyes and said, "You're going to love your baby." After a quick look into my husband's eyes, I knew she was right. We were going to love our baby.

Meeting Hobbs was like meeting the dream I never dreamed. Not because it wasn't a good dream or a beautiful dream, I just didn't know it was possible that I could live this dream. That I could be "one of those" families and be happy. Weren't these the kinds of things that happened to the Mother Teresas and Emily Kingsleys of the world?

When you focus your attention on what *can* be and leave the *cannots* and *never wills* behind, a whole new world appears. It looks a little wild at times and not like everyone else's at all, but *that* is the upside to Down.

ARTICHOKES

~~~~~~~~~~~~~~

KATHY CURTO

U h, miss," he says. "Miss, you okay?" I see black. Nothing
but black. It's happening. I'm dying in the A&P. Blackness
fades. Still alive. Hands clenched on my grocery cart, legs holding me up but frozen hard, stuck to the floor. Tears flow down
my cheeks. Him again. "I mean, can I getcha somethin'? Some
water or somethin'?"

He inches closer and I zero in on his eyes. They are afraid eyes.
I know about that kind. "How 'bout going up by the registers?
There are seats up there and you can sit down for a while?" he says.

I've seen him before, this kid. This produce kid. I remember
now. Two weeks ago I asked him if he had any Swiss chard in the
back and he brought out four heads of bok choy. He reminds me
of my brother, Jack, when he was a boy. Big, fleshy lips. Shaggy,
milk-chocolate hair parted on the side. A smile the size of both
Texas and Mexico. A smile so big you can't help but wonder
what's hiding behind, holding it open.

So, this is where it's happening. In the produce section of the
A&P next to the boy with the afraid eyes. This is where it finally
hits: My mother is dead.

All this time, I worried about Mother's Day and her birthday. I never imagined it would happen almost a year later on a rainy Tuesday in the A&P, with the instrumental version of Tony Orlando's "Knock Three Times" oozing from the speakers above. The new me: hands clenched, holding on to the grocery cart for dear life, weeping.

The artichokes did it. The ones piled high in the bin I stand next to now because my feet are still frozen, stuck to the floor. The ones that are on sale for $2.99 a pound. It's this pile of innocent, misunderstood vegetables that jabs me, jolts me. It's new, this world now. She's gone. So for $2.99 a pound I go from a girl-woman in denial to a self-proclaimed motherless daughter.

My mother. She was a magnificent cook. Not because she measured, diced, chopped, and grated with utter precision but because she didn't. Catherine Pontoriero, Mrs. P. to all my friends, cooked first with her heart and second with her hands. When she fried long, crooked Italian peppers or folded pieces of the hard, moist bread into the raw meat mixture that would become her famous meatballs or even when she browned cheap pieces of pork bone to start her thick Sunday gravy, she was all heart.

"Let me make you something to eat," she'd say to us, her smelly garlic fingers pushing our sweaty bangs away from our eyes.

Or, after I spent a Saturday afternoon riding bikes with my girlfriends, "Come, come," she'd say, directing kitchen traffic with her old wooden spoon, pointing it at the counter stools. "Sit down, girls. Sit down, and you can each taste a meatball."

The smell of her vegetable beef soup lured neighbors to our front stoop, ringing our doorbell and making up stories about needing the name of a plumber. Plastic containers of escarole and beans were brought to my father's gas station and given to customers who tasted it and fell under its spell.

As a senior in high school I had surgery that kept me homebound for one month. The tutor they sent from school told my mother her chicken cutlets were a gift from God. He gained ten pounds by the time my incision healed. And the whole time she cooked, all thirty-one years that we had together, I watched. And back then I watched with eyes that were alive and unafraid, just like hers.

And now it's me who gives containers of my escarole and beans away to people I know and people I don't. My kids love to taste my meatballs fresh from the frying pan, warm with pink juice and the smell of basil swirling out of the fork holes. Pots of soup and chicken cutlets are the first things I think about if a neighbor falls ill.

But the artichokes. I still haven't made the artichokes. She never taught me. Somehow learning how to make the artichokes slipped by and now it's too late. I'm too afraid.

I did love eating them, though. We all did. Biting and scraping off the rough and bitter green meat with our teeth was hard work but amusing, too. I couldn't wait to get to the inside, to the soft breading and to the heart, seasoned with all her basics: fresh garlic, olive oil, basil leaves, bread crumbs, celery.

Making artichokes with my mother never happened. But in our three decades together she nourished more than my body and my bones. My mother offered the most important recipe of all. She fed my soul.

DOES YOUR MOM PLAY DRUMS?

~~~~~~~~~~~~~~~~

MICHELLE CRUZ GONZALES

When I was playing drums in a punk band, rocking out in a tank top and no bra, or just a bra and no tank top, I didn't imagine my favorite performance would be with my ten-year-old son.

For three years, Luis Manuel played piano in his school's variety show. In fifth grade, he decided to play guitar. Guitar was way cooler. He had taught himself to play guitar in like three months, you know, on YouTube: chords, notes, picking, everything. He was going to play a rock song for the variety show; his friend Shane was going to play with him. They began practicing three months before auditions because they didn't want to suck and they had girls to impress.

Then Luis heard a rumor that Shane wasn't going to play with him. When he heard it again, I suggested he find a third person for his act just in case, but he said maybe Shane was just too busy to practice. Then two days before the audition, only two weeks before the actual show, Shane admitted that he was going to be in a dance act with his popular friends instead.

"A dance act? Who in the hell would rather do synchronized dance moves like some boy band over playing actual music?"

It occurred to me right then that, for fifth graders, this variety show had more to do with showcasing your friends than actual talent.

"Do you want to be in their dance act?" I asked.

He rolled his eyes and huffed.

"No, I want to play guitar."

I was relieved.

In tears the night before the auditions, Luis sat on the couch with his Les Paul.

"Maybe I won't do it," he said.

I took a deep breath to hide my panic, not sure why I was so invested; then I told him to play every song he knew. I would help him decide which sounded best. He played "Float On," which needed another guitar; the Beatles' "Blackbird" sounded good, but the picking needed work; and the Weezer song had one really hard chord. When he played Nirvana's "Smells Like Teen Spirit," we both knew it was the one.

Then it hit me. Luis's participation in this event had become our family's way of not being totally invisible. I worked full-time and made an effort to be involved, volunteering in the classroom and going on field trips when I could, but I was not part of the blond moms' crowd or the stay-at-home moms' crowd, or an attending member of the PTA. I was the Chicana with chest tattoos married to a dark-skinned Mexican with an accent. I wasn't going to let some fucking dance routine keep my son from changing his mind about performing in that show.

"I just wish I had someone to play with." He looked dejected.

"You know, I can play that song on drums in my sleep." I tried sounding nonchalant. But it was true, anyone who played rock drums in the nineties had learned to play that song, had wanted to rock as hard as Dave Grohl.

"You want to play with me?" He made a face.

"Look, I know you don't think it's cool to be in an act with your mom, but the auditions are tomorrow; there's no one else."

"Okay," he said, sounding the way you do when you know you're totally out of options.

I wanted to hug him, jump off the couch, plan our outfits, and gush about how fun it was going to be. I restrained myself.

"What if someone teases me?"

"Just say this: 'Does your mom play drums?'"

In pain after dropping his guitar on his big toe the night before, Luis continued to worry that he'd be teased for being in a band with his mom. I knew I had to keep a low profile, tone it down, wear a loose-fitting tank top and a bra, and no flashy makeup. I did put on red lipstick called "Rocker" before leaving the house. I wanted to stand out from the PTA moms and help my son show his friends what real and inspired talent looked like. Getting onstage and playing the drums in front of the entire school without lipstick wouldn't achieve that.

"Next, we have Luis Manuel Peralta playing 'Smells Like Teen Spirit,'" the MC on the other side of the curtain read from the intro we wrote, "and no, that's not his mom on drums." I heard loud laughter, the curtain lurched open, and Luis launched into one of the most recognizable chord progressions in rock and roll, drawing whoops and cheers from the crowd. Then I came in on drums, careful not to hit the snare as hard as I could or move my head wildly as I had in my band Spitboy.

Like we practiced to combat nerves and to help us stay together, we made eye contact across the stage, mother and son. I nodded as we made the transition from the intro to the soft part that follows, and by the time we got to the distinctive chorus, *da, da, da diga, diga, diga, da, da, da,* the crowd was roaring. Luis looked up from his guitar, and I saw his anxiety slip away. Then as we wound down for the big finish, Luis locked eyes with me and smiled wide like he did when I nursed him as a baby. The crowd went wild and Luis's girlfriend swooned in her chair; his friends in the dance act jumped to their feet and clapped; my husband stood at the front of the stage with the camera, grinning; and lots of other husbands rehearsed what they'd say as they approached me afterward. Looking steadily at each other, me and my son punctuated the end of the song, two musicians hitting each beat together. I savored each one, *ba, ba, ba,* knowing that in his eyes, I may never be that cool again.

STEAM POWER

~~~~~~~

HELEN REESE

My older son, Avi, who just became a parent himself a few months ago, calls me up and says:

"Mom. Anne has to go to a conference next month. I don't think I can take care of Ezra by myself. Can you come and help out?"

I grip the phone, willing myself to stay in the present, but feel myself spiraling back in time. It's 1979 and my husband has just returned from a business trip. We're sitting side by side on our threadbare couch, and he's saying, "I'm leaving you. I met someone else."

I'm in shock—terrified, overwhelmed, looking down at my still flat but pregnant belly. Two kids, one not even born yet. How will I do it on my own?

Then I'm flooded with memories of the 24/7 minute-to-minute, hour-to-hour, day-to-day, night-to-night joy, heartbreak, and everything in between of raising two sons with just me, the lone and so often lonely woman in the house. I remember the frenetic rearranging of my schedule whenever the boys were sick, the unrelenting financial worries, and always the exhaustion, the guilt, the strain of being the only parent in our lopsided household.

"So, you'll be able to schedule time off from work, right?" Avi asks, his pleading voice catapulting me back to the present.

"Of course, sweetie," I say. "Of course I'll help."

A month later, I'm on the train to Manhattan feeling excited but anxious about the week ahead. Avi's eyes light up when he sees me, and I can tell he's exhausted and on edge. Ezra's had a cold for a couple of weeks and has a lingering cough. Avi calls the doctor, who examined the baby earlier in the week and saw no cause for concern, and leaves a message that the cough seems to be getting worse and is most troublesome at night. He calls his wife, Anne, and fills her in on every detail of Ezra's condition. They're an extraordinary team, and I marvel again at how seamlessly they work together, and how much they rely on each other's support in taking care of Ezra. I know Avi feels adrift without her this weekend, and I again feel an acute sense of loss because I'll never experience what they have—the shared joy of raising a child, together.

When the doctor calls back twenty minutes later, she recommends the same old tried-and-true remedies I've already reviewed with Avi. When I say, "See, your mother knows a little something about parenting," Avi looks at me in shock.

"What are you talking about, Mom? You always know what to do," he says.

The first night Ezra's cough wakes him up, I'm able to get him back to sleep with a bottle and some gentle rocking. However, the second night he wakes up with a persistent cough and wails inconsolably. Both Avi and I are up, and I can see the concern on his face. He asks me to hold Ezra while he turns on the shower, and we both wait for the steam to fill the bathroom. Avi sits on the toilet seat, holding the whimpering and still coughing baby in his arms. He turns to me—the steam swirling around them—and asks, "Can you take him? I can't handle the heat in here." He hands the baby to me and I pat his back, holding him next to the shower, allowing the steam to work its magic. As Avi's about to leave the bathroom, he turns back to me and says, "I don't know how you ever did this by yourself."

I look at him, stunned. He's never said that to me before. I'm struck by the realization that he never really understood how alone I was until he became a parent himself.

My eyes fill with tears as I say, "I don't know either. Believe me, it never would've been my choice. But I had no choice, so I did the best I could."

He wraps his arms around his son and me, and we stand there for a moment in the steamy bathroom. I feel Ezra's little body relax, as his cough subsides.

IN PRAISE OF THE OTHER MOTHER

~~~~~~~~~~

NANCY DAVIS KHO

People say "Other Woman" like it's a bad thing. But I yearn to be the Other Woman. Because by Other Woman, I mean Other Mother.

Other Mothers are those people in a child's life to whom the kid can go for a fresh perspective, a hot snack, a reminder that things aren't always better on the other side of the cul-de-sac. Other Mothers don't have to be women, and they don't have to be mothers. They must only possess a sympathetic ear, a stocked pantry, and objectivity that can be hard to come by in the emotional fog that sometimes clouds interaction between actual mother and child.

I've always been close to my mom. I was her third child, the kid who rode around on her hip for years and had a permanent berth in the backseat while we drove around in the station wagon to drop off my older siblings at baseball practice and bowling. We didn't clash much, even when I was a teenager.

Yet as much as I love my mom, my Other Mothers were instrumental in helping me make it to adulthood intact. My aunt Noonie, for one. My mom's oldest sister, Noonie was the aunt with whom we got to stay on the rare weekends when Mom and Dad went out of town together. Her main areas of expertise? Astrology, *Star Trek*, and pie baking. She owned my mom in all those categories, and even now if I am back east for a visit, I pray that Noonie has made me a pie and will give me some insight into how the year ahead is going to unfold for us Tauruses. She also made it possible for my parents to have a little romance in their busy lives, which made the lives of their children all the sweeter.

There was the indomitable Mrs. Fitzsimmons next door, whose daughter Bethie was my very best childhood friend. If you added up all the time I spent at the Fitzes' house versus my own during the first ten years of my life, I'd guess it would be a fifty-fifty split. We had cable first, but they had Beatles albums and a top-of-the-line dress-up bin. The merry chaos of their large Irish Catholic family was always entertaining, but sent me back home with a new appreciation for the relative calm of my own house.

In high school my primary Other Mother was Mrs. Moretti, mom of my best friend, Lisa. My mom was put together and stylish, but didn't give a fig for capital *F* fashion. Mrs. Moretti, on the other hand, had three teenage fashion-plate daughters, shopped the fancy stores in town, and read *Vogue* magazine, all of which conferred her authority with which I refused to credit my own mother.

So when I came home one day at seventeen with a Flock of Seagulls–style haircut (shorn short in back, hanging long in front, its geometric planes buttressed by half a can of Aqua Net hair spray), and my mother's reaction was "Please don't go to that butcher again," I naturally vowed to wear it like that forever.

Mrs. Moretti, on the other hand, was effusive with praise

when she first saw my troubling hairstyle. But a few days later, as Lisa and I sat drinking Tab and eating pretzels in the kitchen, Mrs. M slid a page from a fashion magazine across the table to me. It pictured a wholesome, pretty girl with a shoulder-grazing bob, the same shade of blond as mine. Mrs. Moretti said, "That might look nice on you," then turned away to wash some dishes.

And that was the day I started growing out the Shorty Long-sides Haircut, circumventing a lifetime of public embarrassment.

My mother didn't resent these Other Mothers. If anything, she actively encouraged my relationships with them. As a mother of daughters who are twelve and fifteen years old now, I can see exactly why. Some days lay waste to the focus and emotional energy you can muster for a child. Now divide that energy by the number of siblings, and again by the times we have no idea what we are doing. If it weren't for Other Mothers, we actual moms couldn't catch a break.

Other Mothers are genius at ferreting out information that might go unmentioned to the actual parent, like the arrival of a new boyfriend on the scene, or how a kid really feels about play-ing a sport. If you agree ahead of time to exchange key morsels judiciously, like spies from allied nations, this back-channel information gathering can prove extremely useful.

They can also do the heavy lifting in areas where the actual mom has her limits. In a bit of history repeating itself, I found my look and stopped subscribing to fashion magazines in 1995. So when there's a clothing question to be refereed, I tell the girls to ask their über-stylish Other Mother, Andrea. "She'll know," I say, trusting that Andrea is as anti-booty-short and jeggings as I am.

And it is often the Other Mother who gives us solid proof that our kids are maturing into the people we hope they will be. I remind my children to use good manners when they are out in the world without me. But it's not until I get positive confirmation of a good manners sighting from their Other Mother Maria, when they're all at dinner without me, that I can truly believe the lessons have sunk in.

I shamelessly court Other Mother status for the kids in my children's lives. All through middle school my older daughter's best friend would come over to do homework on Mondays because I served her pistachios, a favorite snack that is off-limits at home due to nut allergies in the household. I'll whip up hot cocoa and popcorn at the drop of a hat, and when the kids in my daughter's ninth-grade math class needed a place to work on a class project, I bought all the supplies and heated up a pizza.

In part it's because I genuinely like my daughters' friends. But all those conversations I'm hearing from the next room as I slowly, slowly slice the pizza and stack the dishwasher give me insight into the world in which my children live and the people who surround them there.

And it's the least I can do to pay back the Noonies, the Mrs. Fitzses, and the Mrs. Morettis in my life.

THREE LITTLE LETTERS

LISA ALLEN

H e must have looked funny, standing there in that aisle.

It was 1985 or so, in my small hometown in western Kansas.

In small towns like this one, everyone seems to know everyone else. That's especially true in his case, since he was a sheriff's officer and not exactly shy. People knew him or they knew of him, so even if he'd walked into the Dillon's on Vine Street in jeans and a T-shirt, they'd notice.

But he didn't. Instead he stood in that aisle, likely wearing a bulletproof vest under his polyester uniform shirt. Radio strapped to his shoulder, holster hanging around his waist, badge pinned above his pocket. With his Tom Selleck mustache and his shock of bright red hair, he didn't exactly fit in the health and beauty section, much less the feminine care aisle.

Yet there he was. I can still see him now, in my mind, as I imagine he looked that night. His left thumb hooked inside his pants pocket, the other probably alternately scratching his cheek and cupping his chin. He still does that now, too, even though it's almost thirty years later. It's one of his deep-in-thought gestures, like doodling as he talks, sketching out details of a story as he speaks them.

I imagine the look that must have washed over his face as he stood there, surveying the dizzying array of options—light, medium, heavy, mini, maxi, scented, and unscented—and probably wondered why things are never easy with women.

Having teenage girls as a single dad couldn't have been easy. When my parents first divorced, we followed tradition and stayed with our mom. I still remember the first night he picked the three of us up for "his night" after he'd moved out of our house on Marjorie Drive.

We sat, waiting, on the couch in the living room. The same couch we'd sat on a few weeks before, when the people we called parents told us that Dad was leaving and we'd be staying there, with Mom. The bell rang and I remember thinking how odd it was, that kids and friends and family traipsed in and out of our house all day without ringing the bell but our dad—our DAD—was asking for permission to come in.

He didn't come in, not past the threshold anyway. I remember how he was dressed: one of those fab, dressy, seventies-inspired button-down shirts that I rarely saw him wear. Hair combed and looking like he did for church, which I also thought was odd. I always saw him in work clothes, which were streaked with paint and splattered with putty and dirt. When he wasn't on duty he juggled countless part-time jobs to take care of everyone.

But that night was special. He took us out for dinner and to the one and only movie I've ever seen with him in a theater: *Splash*. I remember Tom Hanks and Daryl Hannah, but what I remember most is that he bought us popcorn. It was almost like a party but of course it wasn't happy. It was just the beginning of a new normal.

We moved with my mom from place to place, but he was always the constant in the chaos. Even after working the 11-to-7 shift (11:00 at night to 7:00 a.m., not the other way around), he would pull into the driveway of whichever place Mom had decided to call home for a while to pick me up and take me to school. After I climbed up into the passenger seat of his embarrassingly huge and loud yellow Blazer and closed the door, he'd hand me a Styrofoam plate, rimmed with drips of condensation and filled with pancakes or eggs or both. He knew without ever having walked into the kitchen of Mom's place that the only thing in our fridge was probably Mountain Dew and eggs no one would cook.

Eventually we went to live with him, which is where we belonged from the beginning. When I was young, I didn't see that for the true gift that it was, and I didn't realize just how challenging it must have been for a divorced man to buck the trend and fight for custody of three girls.

It was common practice to automatically grant favor to the mother in custody issues. Traditional wisdom said that kids belong with their mother.

A traditional mom would have gone to Dillon's and shopped the feminine care aisle for her daughters.

Ours didn't.

But he did.

Webster's defines "mother," the noun, simply as a female parent. For a title so charged with emotion, the definition is surprisingly sterile and succinct. A parent is defined as one who begets or brings forth offspring. It's the birth certificate and the shared physical characteristics; my red hair from him, my prominent nose from her. I've inherited both, without choosing or acting or even wanting.

Dictionary.com defines "mothering" as a transitive verb: to acknowledge oneself the author of; assume as one's own; to care for or protect like a mother; to act maternally toward.

What a difference between the noun and the verb. Tack on three little letters and the willingness to brave the feminine care aisle between traffic stops and drug busts, and you can change a life.

The verb is everything we imagine and hope for the noun to be. It encompasses acceptance, family, nurturing, and love. The verb has nothing to do with biology or body parts but everything to do with heart. It is the tough-love conversations and the tender moments right before he walks you down the aisle and the shoulder you lean on during your own divorce.

The verb is bucking convention, rewriting tradition, and learning how to answer the tough questions, like the difference between mini and maxi. It's been quite some time since my dad has needed to make a grocery store run on my behalf, but that doesn't matter. Because of his willingness to step up, step in, and stick around, he's shown me that it's not what we're given that matters. It's what we give.

THE TINY BRIDGE-MAKER

JENNIFER NEWCOMB MARINE

"All I know is, when we have a baby, I don't want her to see it, hold it, or have anything to do with it. She just needs to stay away!" Those were the sentiments of Carol, my children's stepmother.

Luckily, I wasn't around to hear this.

Because "she" meant . . . me.

But now, here I was, lodged in the green velvet chair of my living room, next to a snazzy new diaper bag full of jammies, clean diapers, and an extra bottle. Teething rings were cooling in the freezer. My daughters, Sophie and Madeleine, were happily tucked away in the family room, watching a movie.

Six-month-old Jacob was leaning heavily back into the crook of my arm, drinking from a bottle; big, blue eyes framed by long lashes, looking intently at my face. I gently combed his fine blond hair away from his forehead with the tips of my fingers and felt my heart catch. His hands tightly pressed down over mine on the bottle as if to say, *You are not allowed to move,* and he swallowed steadily and loudly.

Quite a leap from there to here. And certainly where I never imagined I'd find myself: babysitting the child of my ex-husband David and his second wife.

I found out later that Carol's worries about kids started from the very beginning of their relationship. She wanted children—but he already had two (and a vasectomy meant they would most likely need to adopt). If it were up to him alone, he would have been "happy with what he had," but once he understood how important it was to her to have more, it became a priority for him, too.

Privately though, Carol fretted that he wouldn't love their baby as much as his own. What if he always ending up feeling more connected to his first daughters?

And life as the other "hands-on parent" made it even easier for her to daydream about how much better it'd be with her own child.

It was the Stepmother's Curse in action—you work your ass off to win over the children, to try and bring structure and order and harmony to their lives in that woman's-overview kind of a way, and what do you get in return? They fall down and wail for their mother. From her vantage point as a woman longing to be a mother, we, the parents, slacked off on some of the hard work, like consistency and consequences; yet reaped all the goodies, like instantaneous forgiveness, unconditional love and affection, and boundless, unreasonable enthusiasm.

My brain had kicked into overdrive when they started dating, too. When I'd heard they were actually going to marry, a part of me panicked. It's bad enough knowing that your children are going to be exposed on a continuing basis to someone you barely know or approve of, but when you think of her and your ex adding to their lives—a whole new family unit that your kids now have to integrate with—truly, the mind boggles.

She and I were like wary dogs circling each other in the beginning—distrustful, nervous, suspicious. We had no good reason to think well of each other. She was young, beautiful, artistically and domestically gifted in spades. I, well, I was the older, haggard single mother, not so full of promise and the blush of youth anymore, but trying to make do, nevertheless.

Bit by bit, we got to a neutral, casual place, one that you might reserve for neighbors you wave hello to in the morning.

And gradually it took. Still, when it came down to cave-woman concerns about my clan and theirs, all those efforts at social lubrication flew out the window. From that base of cool and efficient self-interest, I flatly didn't care what Carol wanted; matter of fact, I could barely remember.

When it became apparent that Carol and David were now going to add to their family in earnest, my first line of thinking was, great, but how is this going to affect us financially, on a survival level—our bottom line? Is responsibility for the girls going to fall lopsidedly my way?

It doesn't make any sense, but even against the backdrop of such thinking, our friendship continued to grow and became more than superficial chitchat during drop-offs and pickups. I discovered the person beneath the role, like a wax figure slowly coming to life, and actually looked forward to talking to her. We connected on the phone in occasional marathon phone sessions and I marveled at the both of us: Look! We're becoming real, honest friends!

And yet, on another level, it stunk, because now I had a choice to make.

The stronger our friendship, the harder it was to return to my own selfish priorities; I was well aware that a new child might mean something "negative" for our household. It was an odd conundrum. If I was going to let Carol in—really reach out to her with acceptance and support, just the way I would a "normal" friend—I'd have to let go of the last vestiges of that us-versus-them mentality and turn it into a collective us.

I watched David and Carol go through the emotional roller coaster of trying to adopt with one agency—and failing—and my heart softened. When a young couple finally picked them out, the girls were ecstatic, and I was surprised to find that I was truly excited, too.

Now the waiting game began. The birth mother still had two months to go until she delivered. Would she change her mind at the end?

Finally, the baby was born.

David and Carol spent most of the weekend at the hospital, wanting to spend as much time as possible with the baby. We were all on pins and needles, wondering if the birth mother would finally sign the papers during the seventy-two hours she had to change her mind about handing over her new, scrunchy-faced, beautiful baby boy to Carol and David, who wanted him so much, and to Sophie and Madeleine, who would gain an instant baby brother.

I was asked to bring the girls to the hospital only hours after Jacob was born so they could see him. I looked into Carol's eyes with humbled awe as she handed me the baby to hold in the rocking chair, fighting hard to blink back tears.

Can you imagine?

Jacob came home on his second day in this world to live with his new family.

I still wasn't sure how I fit into this picture, and honestly, now that Carol and I had so strongly connected in a way that even I didn't understand, I was hesitant to step on her toes at all.

I hung back and let her take the lead.

As she explained later, when she started thinking of the baby as not just hers, but as Madeleine's and Sophie's too, then her feelings about "sharing" him with me started to change. I began to love this spunky, outgoing little boy; I began to feel connected, to look forward to seeing him.

Looking back, I can see that widening a net that included me could not have been forced. It was an evolutionary process that was slowly and sometimes painstakingly (emphasis on pain) built upon forgiveness, mutual understanding, and wanting to build a bigger sense of family for the girls and now for Jacob.

We worked on creating warmth and peace, and eventually, even love between our households. Small presents went both ways between the adults; burned CDs, desserts, birthday cards, a nice shirt the other person might like that was just hanging in our closet.

And somewhere during those first few seasons of Jacob's life, one of the greatest honors in the world was bestowed upon me: I was made his honorary aunt. It is one of my proudest titles and most treasured, unusual gifts. I am acutely aware of its rarity, and that makes it even more special.

Jacob recently celebrated his third birthday, and indeed, he feels just exactly like my nephew. I look forward to watching his life unfold and hope it's a long, rich, and happy one.

Little did I know, years ago, how much this little person would come to mean to me, or how powerfully he would pull us all closer together.

BOTTLE CAPS, APPLE TREES, AND HOPE

~~~~~~~~~

SHEILA QUIRKE

Sometimes a bottle cap can change your life.

When my daughter, Donna, was in the thick of her cancer treatment, we were blessed with tremendous support. Our family cooked for us, cleaned for us, laundered for us, and supported us so we could support our girl.

During that time, despite all the help we had, I remember just pining for simple things. *I* wanted to do the grocery shopping. I wanted to fold our socks the way *I* wanted to fold our socks and was embarrassed when my undies had been folded by someone else. I wanted to do the dishes. It's hard to imagine the simple things you take for granted when your world is turned upside down and inside out. That pining for the ability to just simply run our household by myself always made me feel like an ungrateful jerk. I'm sorry, Grandma! I'm sorry, Papa! I'm sorry, Auntie!

One blessed day, I got the chance to do dishes. In the midst of chaos and uncontrollable circumstances, having a task with a beginning, middle, and end feels like pure bliss. It makes sense, you know? The kitchen starts out with crumbs and dirty dishes and coffee rings under mugs left on the counter. Twenty minutes later, the sink is empty, the crumbs are gone, the counters are clear, and the dish rack is full. This is a simple pleasure of life, if you can get past the oppression of its constancy.

So the cap. As I was clearing dishes into the soapy sink that day years ago, I found an iced tea bottle. I rinsed it out and saw its companion cap. I noticed the words on it. It says, "Even if I knew that tomorrow the world would go to pieces, I would still plant my apple tree." Huh. Then, Whoa. Followed by, Wow.

The quote is falsely attributed to Martin Luther King, Jr. These words were actually spoken by Martin Luther of the Protestant Reformation Luthers. Hmmm . . . Sixteenth-century theologian and twentieth-century civil rights activist—apparently, Snapple doesn't sweat the details. Anyway.

When I read these words, I knew that *my* world would shortly be going to pieces. I knew that my firstborn would die. I knew this intellectually and emotionally. It is crippling to have this knowledge about your child. Just typing that sentence made me burst into tears, leading my son to offer me the green car he was playing with at my feet. He knows full well what his mother's tears are usually about.

That knowledge, crippling and brutal as it is, is like all knowledge. It is power. Because of that knowledge, I had the power to say good-bye. Because of that knowledge, I had the power to try and prepare Donna to die. Because of that knowledge, I had the power to try and prepare myself for Donna to die.

We had the opportunity to plant those apple trees knowing what we were doing. Martin Luther's words are, in essence, all about what I call "choosing hope." Despite knowing the end of the world is nigh, plant those apple trees, people, he advises. Hope for something better, a different outcome, eternal salvation, whatever it is that brings you comfort and solace.

I am so grateful for the proverbial apple trees we planted. Just two months before Donna died, I wrote of our choices inspired by hope, "*These* are our apple trees. And my latest hope is that these trees will sustain us when our world does go to pieces. That these trees will feed us and shade us and shelter us from the inevitable storms that will be."

Yes, there have been storms. Some days stormier than others. Some days the rain falls steadily in our hearts and out our eyes even though the sun is shining brightly outside. But those apple trees have done exactly what I hoped they would do.

Choosing hope has and continues to feed us, shade us, and shelter us from the storm of grief over losing our child, our Donna. Those apple trees, the decision to choose hope, most meaningfully benefit our beloved sons.

Choosing hope and planting those apple trees both allow us to keep our roots, the memories of our dear Donna, and grow and reach and still produce the sweet, sweet fruit of mothering.

PREGNANT AGAIN

~~~~~~~~~~~~~~~

EDWARD McCANN

W hen I found out I was pregnant with you," Mom told me, "pregnant again, for the sixth time—I wanted to walk into the ocean until my hat floated."

So. It turns out my conception was not deliberate.

By the time I was conceived in late June 1962, there were already five children at home, ranging in age from a brand-new high school graduate to a toddler of fifteen months. I am the third son and my parents' youngest child, the one my mother called her "caboose," the last car on the freight train of my family.

Mom was forty-two and my father nearing fifty when I was born. Now ninety-three, wheelchair-bound, and widowed for as long as she was married, Mom has often told me how much she loves and appreciates me—how "God surely knew what he was doing" when he sent me so late in her life. Still, I can't forget that sense of desperation she once expressed, the hopelessness behind even that momentary suicidal impulse, the image of a pregnant, Irish Catholic Queens housewife drowning herself like Virginia Woolf, perhaps weighting herself down, as Virginia did, with rocks in her coat pockets, and with me—or, rather, the cluster of cells that might have become me—in her womb.

The idea is especially disturbing because it's so easy to imagine, and Mom wouldn't have had to travel very far before she got her feet wet; Broad Channel, the provincial island town where my family lived, was surrounded by water on all sides—an anomaly, more fishing village than New York City, with Jamaica Bay and the nearby Atlantic always present in the salt air, the scream of the gulls, the fog that sometimes rose up around us.

No child wants to imagine his or her conception, but I do, just this once: I count months backward from my birthday. I use the Internet to check historic weather conditions, moon cycles, and tide charts. And then I travel back in time, becoming a fly on the wall on that mild spring night as my soon-to-be parents climbed the stairs of their house on the Boulevard. The children are all in their beds. Dad, feeling frisky, pats Mom's rump as they climb the stairs, a signal she knows well and which I imagine fills her with dread.

George and Mildred are not hoping to produce another child, another mouth to feed. But though Mom is tired and premenopausal, Dad has his needs and Mom her wifely duties— duties her mother informed her about shortly before Mildred's wedding some twenty years past. Still a blushing teen, Mildred sat stock-still with her hands covering her mouth as she finally learned the long overdue facts of life and the indignities she would have to endure as a married woman.

A light breeze off the bay ruffles the polyester sheers of my parents' screened bedroom windows. By the dim light of the moon, George takes his pleasure behind a locked door beneath the crucifix that hangs above their bed. Mildred, meanwhile, closes her eyes and says a silent decade of the rosary, a meditation that transports her away from her body for as long as it takes.

My parents married young, created a home and a family, and they shared their happiness and sorrows. Yet it sometimes seemed to me that Mildred's life—her marriage and her six children—was something that just happened to her, and perhaps wasn't the life she might have chosen if she'd ever believed she had a choice.

"I wanted to walk out into the ocean until my hat floated."

Pregnant again. I can only imagine the different, perhaps sunnier landscape into which Mom's first child was born, the time before my mother's life became an unending laundry cycle, the days unfurling one after the other like an endless potato peel. And then I recall my childhood visits to Far Rockaway beach— the Irish Riviera—where Mom taught me to swim and (eventually) how to relax enough to lie back and ride atop the waves like she did, eyes closed and hands clasped behind her head, her face turned toward the sun.

BECOMING DA MOMMY

M. PENNY MANSON

Last night I got the phone call every daughter dreads. "Hello, Mrs. Manson? Your mother coldcocked a member of the senior day-care staff."

"No, you must be mistaken," I say. "My mom is a ninety-one-year-old great-grandmother." "Yes," comes the reply, "we know, but she still has a great right hook." I was very worried. This behavior could mean Mom would get kicked out of the adult day-care program she goes to three times a week. We both need it. Her, for socialization and mental stimulation, and me, for a break from caring for her and my peace of mind.

Today the squeaking door announced Mom up and ready to begin her day. Slipping in before she can put on her robe, wander into our bedroom or down the hall, I whisper, "Good morning." The Parkinson's symptoms have given my husband a rough night and I don't want to wake him.

Mom looks at me, tilts her head to one side, and says, "Am I asleep or are you?"

I sigh. "I am not asleep, because you are not asleep." She sits on her bed and her legs swing. This visual cue means the aggressive state from the adult day care has been reduced to anxiety. She is subdued for the moment but I am not sure how long it will last. The Xanax, now increased to three pills a day, has not made her a zombie, but she is not herself. I'm not sure who she is, but she isn't my mom—she just looks like her.

Your folks might say, "Don't sacrifice yourself for me. Find a good place for me and don't feel guilty about it. Do it and go on with your life." I wish she had written me a letter saying those things. Because now it is not the face of my mom that I see, but the face of a tear-stained two-year-old, saying "I'm sorry, I won't be bad, don't send me away," and it breaks my heart.

"The Sugar," or type 2 diabetes, ran in my family, claiming first my oldest brother and then my sister. In 2007 Mom buried her firstborn son before his sixty-fifth birthday. When diagnosed, my sister started self-destructive behavior. She stopped communicating with family and friends and Mom feared the worst. Those fears were realized when my sister was found dead in her apartment four days before she would have been sixty-seven, two weeks before Mom's eighty-sixth birthday. I flew home to help my mother bury a second child a year and a half after the first.

My heart was heavy with loss and this awareness; for me to take care of Mom, as her dementia worsened, she would have to move to California. In addition to caring for my husband, I would begin caring for someone whose unstoppable energy had started a final game of hide-and-seek.

Packing a life in a bag taxes the back; packing a grieving spirit taxes everything and everyone. I watched the take-care-of-everything, handle-anything spirit drain from my mom. She spoke with longing of having a bath, her apartment having only a shower stall. The night before I moved my mother from St. Louis, while at my cousin's house, I suggested a warm bath, thinking it might help her relax and feel better. I helped her get into the tub and asked if she wanted me to stay and bathe her. I rose, expecting her to shoo me out when she was settled. "Please stay," she whispered. I turned to look at her. That moment something shifted between us. My strong, wise, independent mother needed me to be the strong, wise one. The woman who had held my hands needed me to soothe her.

They say a child will wear you to a nub faster than anything, but no toddler could be more demanding than this giant child of mine. I have become da mommy. I, the child who never had a child, now have this childlike spirit to care for and love. I have been drafted into this club of caregivers that no one volunteers to join and no one is eager to leave because the only way out is through the gate marked "Cemetery."

I am tired but not sorry. No matter how frustrating, difficult, or filled with challenges these days may be, this will never change: She is my mommy, and I treasure each day I have with her.

MOTHERING THROUGH THE STORM

~~~~~~~~~~

REBECCA ANDERSON-BROWN

Do you remember the TV ad likening depression to being followed around by a little storm cloud? How quaint. Picture this instead: One of those little creeks that's pretty low most of the time. So low that a sapling has grown up in the middle of it; about four feet tall; tall enough to hold a small swallows' nest. It's lovely, really; until a storm comes. The storm itself is like storms usually are; it's the aftermath. The little creek has turned into a raging river, the kind that scrapes mud from the banks, that threatens to rip the sapling out by its roots. The tree is whipping all over, bending, on the edge of breaking and then you see that there are three baby birds in the nest. Three tiny swallows calling out for their mother. Their mother, who is trapped on the other side of the bank, is unable to save her sons from the raging water.

I am that sapling. I am also that bird. This is mothering with depression.

I diagnosed myself with depression when I was twenty-three; my physician agreed after I had presented her with the evidence and I was then properly medicated and sent on my way. This was the beginning of a journey that I had no idea would play such an important and painful role in my life from then on. It wasn't until I was pregnant with my first child that depression became a true force to be reckoned with, set up a home base and declared war. The healthy-baby police recommended that antidepressants not be taken while pregnant and since I was going to have the world's most perfect and pure child, I could surely live without them for nine months, because after all I was feeling fine anyway and they were just "happy pills," weren't they?

No. Martin Luther King Day, 2002. I sat huddled in the corner of my bedroom, sobbing, trying desperately to disappear and my husband trying desperately to find something that would help me. I was terrified, swallowed up by darkness, hopelessness, utterly convinced that the baby growing inside me not only deserved better, but might not even make it, so thick and poisonous were my thoughts. He called my OB. Emergency appointments were made. Therapists were contacted, prescriptions called in and restarted immediately. And I sat in the corner and wept.

Why? That's the thing about depression. There is no why. My husband and well-meaning loved ones can ask, their voices coated with concern, "But what are you sad about?" But there is nothing. There is nothing specific and everything all at once. In the last ten years I've learned a lot about what it means to have a mental illness. Because that's what it is, a mental illness. As a mother you could tell me that I had almost any other chronic illness and I could be braver than with this. High blood pressure, fine. Diabetes, okay. I don't in any way mean to belittle other illnesses, but there are few other illnesses that come with this threat: they could take away my children. That's the reason you try not to go to "mental illness." I've seen the movies, both well done and TV made. There always seems to be shock treatments and shuffling slippers and terrified visiting children. You hear "mental illness" and you think of mothers who have drowned their children because voices told them to do it. You think, no, that can't be me. I can't be one of them. I love my children with my whole heart. It makes me sick to my stomach to hear about these crazy mothers. I can't bear to think about it.

But then you do. In the quiet of night, in your darkest, loneliest moments, some voice that you can't turn off tells you exactly what you don't want to hear. They loved their children too, but they were mentally ill. You are mentally ill. The quiet voice won't stop pointing out the similarities, no matter how long and hard you beg it to stop.

So I am vigilant. I take my medicine. I see a shrink. I see a therapist. I pay attention to how I feel and when I feel the world closing in I try to take a breath and push back. My husband, Tom, is the most perfect ally I can imagine. After ten years and three children, he can sense when I need an emotional vacation. He will encourage me to take entire weekends to disappear just to refind myself. Tom has saved my life and sanity on many an occasion. Which I know is not what he signed up for when we were nineteen.

But just because I'm so damn self-aware, the goddess of depression, doesn't mean I still don't fall prey to its grasp. That's the scariest part of it for me. I know what to look for. I know how it feels and I know what to do, but somehow, it seeps in through some invisible cracks in my strong, competent exterior and suddenly

I'm shocked to find myself consumed by the most terrifying question of all: What's the point?

When you come upon me in that moment, you will know. My eyes will have a hopeless cast and a kind of emptiness that's not familiar. I'll be smiling, but you'll be able to tell quickly that it barely cracks the surface. I'll be paying attention to my children in only the most basic way and even though I will still be loving them with all my heart, I won't be able to show them. And that will kill me. There is an awareness, as if I am watching from above, looking down at myself, seeing this strange, sad woman robotically care for her children and wondering why. The feeling is what I imagine a discarded piece of clothing must feel like. Thrown haphazardly down onto the floor, unable to move on until someone picks it up.

Pick me up. Please. Pick me up because I will not be able to ask you to. I will not know until you have done it that I needed to be picked up. That's the worst part of depression; we often don't know how bad it was until we're through its fog.

As if I don't have enough to worry about or obsess over, if I leave room in my brain, it will jump to the future. Not my future, but my boys'. This depression, this mental illness, has a strong genetic component, and in every depressive state I've entered, guilt has been waiting to meet me at the door. "Look," he always says, "look what you have given your children." This thought alone crushes me.

Any parent at all wants their child to live a healthy life free of as much darkness and despair as possible. And here I am, handing out darkness and despair along with blue eyes and short stature. The guilt is deep and thick and it will pull me under like quicksand if I let it grab my ankle. The key, the hardest part, is not to give it anything to grab. My therapist has told me that my boys are lucky because I know, I understand, and I watch. These words are my talisman when it gets dark, when I can find nothing but shame to pile on my back for bringing these three perfect boys into this world tainted with my sadness.

The darkness and despair may have grabbed at me over the years and still try to pull me down once in a while when the fog rolls in, but I will do everything I can to keep them from getting those boys. My boys and I, we talk about feelings, discuss the emotion, and further, what to do with it. When my adolescent's eyes are downcast and his brow furrowed, I'll sidle up to him and gently ask, "What's up?" When my little boys give me the look that says they're worried about something very real or even just perceived, it's time to pull them into my lap and whisper into the soft skin of their necks. There are many hugs, many kisses. Love is a freely given commodity and I believe this will be part of what saves them.

Because you know what happens to that sapling over time, in the creek? It grows. It grows into a tall, strong tree that withstands any storm that rushes at it.

I am that mother bird trying to get to her sons, but I am also that tree.

WAITING FOR MY KIDS TO WISH ME A HAPPY MOTHER'S DAY

MEGGAN SOMMERVILLE

~~~~~~~~

Once a year, on a Sunday in May, we stop what we are doing and take one day to celebrate our moms (though most would agree that one day is not nearly enough). Mother's Day is when we moms want to be pampered and, for our day-in and day-out, year-round hard work, to be recognized by our children and our families.

The month of May is filled with retail sales and brunch specials everywhere you turn. They are all geared to pamper the mom in your life. You walk into any grocery store and you are bombarded with buckets of fresh-cut flowers, wine, and boxes of chocolates all targeting those kids and fathers that are scrambling for that last-minute gift for Mom. Not a day goes by in that month that I don't hear a commercial on the radio or open my mailbox and see a reminder of something as a mom.

Many women at this time of year struggle with a multitude of emotions. Some women have lost a son or daughter on the battlefield, some have lost a child to disease, and many others have had to say good-bye to their child due to an accident. There are many more women that have lived their lives and have never known the unique challenge and joy of raising a child.

But for women like me, this day is very different. You see, my two kids don't call me Mom.

In 2010, a lot of things changed in my life. I went from male to female. I went from Mark to Meggan. I went from a son to a daughter. But one thing still has not changed. There is one thing that makes this time of year extremely difficult to deal with. My kids, as much as they have moved forward, adjusted to the new normal, and grown from the whole experience, still do one thing that only they can change. They still call me Dad.

We have had our talks, and emotional talks at that. They have shared their concerns and fears, and I have reassured them that I am in no way trying to take the place of my ex-wife as their mom. I have also added that there are a lot of kids that have two moms.

The kids and I agree that the Dad title really isn't appropriate anymore, especially in public. We have tried to find something else, anything, they can call me other than that masculine title.

I understand that my kids have had a difficult time dealing with their dad disappearing and a woman taking his place. They have done a great job changing over the pronouns from the masculine to the feminine, but this one title and the parental role they see that I have in their life still hasn't changed and, to be realistic, may never fully change.

I have done all I can to ease their transition in the last three years. As any good parent, I have learned from my mom and I try my best to equip my children with what they need to face changes and challenges in their life, conquer obstacles, and face life with strength and determination. Right now, whatever the wall is that keeps them from seeing me as one of their "moms" is just too high. In this strange world they have been thrown into, "Dad" is that anchor to the past.

At this point you might ask, "Why don't you and your children just keep celebrating Father's Day?"

My response to that is Father's Day is a masculine-driven day for *men*! Have you looked at me lately? Do you know me, even one bit about me? I'm a woman, *not* a man. I am a mom, not a dad.

Since I have never felt like a man, Father's Day for all those years was something that haunted me. I smiled and truly enjoyed whatever gifts my children got me. Barbecue tools aren't just for men, you know. But inside, my heart sank each time anything masculine was ever attributed to me.

I didn't have to physically give birth to my children to be their mom. Every woman who has opened her heart and adopted a child knows that all too well. Being a mom is the heart you show every day. Being a mom is taking every ounce of love in your soul and spreading it over your kids. It's cuddling them when they are sick or tired. It's sending prayers ahead of them, to places they haven't even imagined yet.

As difficult as it is, I can do nothing more but continue to be patient, caught between two special days for parents.

A bright glimmer of change came this year when my now-eighteen-year-old daughter came to me and said, "Oh I forgot to tell you, you're gonna be a grandma."

GULP!

After I choked back the shock, I remembered that she was

talking about the computerized baby she was going to be assigned for her child development class. We talked about all the details that it was going to involve, and the whole time my mind fixated on one word that my daughter had used—"grandma." My heart was melting. She had taken another step forward.

As much as we want to keep our children small forever, they have this nasty habit of getting older, and as they do, our relationships with them change. Through the years our relationships grow deeper and more complex. I have already seen this happen between my daughter and me.

My hope and prayer is that someday, somewhere in our future, that last vestige of maleness still haunting me is left in the past. I truly hope that when my children are blessed with their own kids, my daughter, future daughter–in-law, and I can celebrate Mother's Day together.

THE CHILDREN ATE MY GRATITUDE

~~~~~~~~~~~~~~~~

ANN IMIG

M om? Can I have one?"

I looked up from my computer, expecting to see Elliott holding the pack of gum I keep in my purse, or the new bag of potato chips from the pantry. He had nothing in his hands.

"One of what?" I asked, peering around my computer screen.

He pointed down on my desk to a small silver box originally intended to hold playing cards. It had once belonged to my Grandma Jo.

"Max had one," he continued.

"What do you mean, he had one?" I asked, no closer to understanding what my son was begging for, nor why he'd interrupted my work.

"He ate one yesterday." Elliott opened the box and started reaching inside. I shooed him away.

"Son, that's paper. Your brother ate paper?? We don't eat paper."

"But Max had one!" Elliott's pincers aimed again toward the tiny strips of paper inside the silver box.

You see, on my therapist's advice, I had taken to practicing gratitude—*practicing* gratitude. Not just feeling grateful but making it an active verb. So I took a self-help book suggestion, using a special box to stow the names of people or things that made me feel grateful. When I remembered to, I took a moment to jot down a little gift from my day in the name of a helpful colleague, dear friend, or one of my professional idols doing their part to nudge me along my path. I wrote mini-prayers of thanks, like "working body," "warm house," or "Mark Ruffalo," on slivers of Post-it notes, and added them to the box. After some days, the box contained a veritable potpourri of slips of paper extolling my loved ones, happy places, and peaceful moments. Maybe snack mix is a better metaphor, considering that my children had apparently been noshing on them.

The children ate my gratitude.

Having already eaten all of my bread, cereal, peanut butter, ice cream, minutes, patience, and sleep, one by one the boys were snacking on their nana, my mentor Deb, above-zero windchills, their daddy, my girlfriends, dry martinis, our house cleaners, and my sanity.

Over the years, I've pried coins, Legos, and marbles from my kids' mouths, but with a seven- and ten-year-old, I assumed we were safely past that stage. The boys dress themselves, and siren songs from the bathroom no longer define my days. Max creates custom rainbow-loom action figures, and Elliott graduated into the black belt training program that requires a uniform complete with an adult-protection apparatus and nunchucks.

They still play with Legos, improvising spoken dialogue, and like me to sing to them at night (while I scream, "BODIES TO YOURSELVES," in between lines of "Good Night, Irene"). Their made-up jokes and curious questions fill us up far more than they deplete us (unless you count rides to extracurricular activities, money, or arguments over Minecraft minutes).

"Son," I told him. "You guys are old enough to know not to eat paper. The answer is no, and don't ask me again."

They didn't ask me again.

Only just the other day I noticed the lid of Grandma Jo's box ajar, and a little confetti labeled "cucumber eye cream" dangling precariously over the side. Who or what got plucked from their bed of silver and deposited into my kids' esophagi, I'll never know. Just in case, I sat down and added a new "Max" and an "Elliott" to the collection.

I think I'd better go count my blessings.

RAISED BY LESBIANS

On My Makeup-Free Mom,
My Fashion-Challenged Moments, and Raising
a Disney Daughter in a Feminist World

~~~~~~~~~~~~~

JENNIFER WEINER

The best present I ever got was given to me in seventh grade, for Chanukah. It was from my friend Roseanne McFarland, and it probably cost all of five dollars. It was a tiered plastic tray of Revlon makeup: two discs of blush, six rectangles of eye shadow, a blush brush, and two tiny plastic-and-foam paddles for applying the eye shadow.

It was the first makeup I'd ever owned. More than that, it was, quite possibly, the first makeup that had ever been in our house in suburban Connecticut.

My mother did not wear makeup. Not any makeup, ever. She did not own a single pair of high heels; she rarely wore dresses or skirts. On her bedroom wall hung a picture of my mother in her twenties, on a trip to New Orleans, pregnant with me, that my father had taken, with a quote from Christian Dior underneath: "Happiness is the secret to all beauty. There is no beauty without happiness."

My mom spent—and still spends—her days in elastic-waist

cropped cotton pants, Birkenstock-style sandals, and loose tunics in primary colors. On a good day, the pants will be pink and the shirt will be brown. On a bad day, the pants are bright red and the shirt is . . . yellow. "You look like squeeze bottles of ketchup and mustard," one of my brothers would say . . . and my mother would laugh and agree and head, barefaced, out the door.

In retrospect, when she came out of the closet at fifty-four, announcing that she'd fallen in love with a woman she'd met in the swimming pool of the West Hartford JCC—where I've never been back in the water—none of us should have been surprised. The signs were everywhere . . . or rather, the signs were nowhere. The lack of long hair and high heels and lipstick. The collection of sport-specific sneakers that took up space in the closet where another woman's stilettos and jeweled ballet flats might have gone. The carved wood jewelry box that went unopened for months at a time, the XXL men's T-shirts worn in lieu of nightgowns . . . you didn't need to be Angela Lansbury to figure that one out (but, in our defense, it's sometimes tricky to distinguish between lesbian and New Englander. Things that are tip-offs in other parts of the world—L.L.Bean anoraks, short hair, and Subarus—are common to both groups).

Growing up with a mom who could not have cared less left me, shall we say, fashion challenged. Not only did my mother not care how she looked, she didn't much care how her kids looked, either, as long as our clothes were seasonally appropriate and not visibly dirty or ripped. She was not the kind of mom who delighted in dressing her daughters in frills and pink. My sister and I wore our hair yanked back into sensible ponytails that my mother made each morning, yanking a green-handled plastic brush through the tangles, ignoring our screams of pain. We wore pants and shirts purchased from the clearance rack at Marshalls, where my mother would go, dutifully, once every few months, when one of us had outgrown our current size. "This'll fit someone," she'd mutter, grabbing pants and shirts by the handful and tossing them into the cart. One unfortunate year, Marshalls had a sale on long-sleeved shirts with a single letter on front. The letter was, I guessed, meant to stand for the kid's name, and Marshalls had made a bulk buy of the shirts with letters that hadn't sold. I'll never forget my mom presenting my then-six-year-old brother Joe with a shirt with a G sewn on the front.

"G?" said Joe, looking puzzled. "My name starts with J."

"It's G for Great Kid," said my mother, undeterred . . . and poor Joe wore that shirt for an entire school year.

Needless to say, I was not a girl who grew up tottering around in Mom's heels, with bright circles of rouge on her cheeks, practicing at beauty . . . I just knew, instinctively, that when it came to clothes and hair, I was doing it wrong. I could, at the very least, identify the things the other girls carried—the brands they wore, the bags they had—and try to get them, and hope it would help. I was a girl who begged and pleaded and saved her own money to buy a pair of Tretorn sneakers with the pink triangle, in spite of my mother's shrugs and insistence that they were really no different, and no better, than sneakers from the Marshalls sales rack. Pink Tretorn sneakers, I was positive, were all that separated me from the popular girls, the ones with the wooden-handled Bermuda bags with reversible covers that buttoned on and off, with Fair Isle sweaters and Jordache jeans, who shopped at Benetton and The Limited. Even though I was beginning to suspect that it was my personality, not my wardrobe, that ultimately separated me from those girls, I felt duty bound to try.

It took me years—way longer than it should have—to figure out clothes and hair and makeup, to learn that eyebrows could be plucked and shaped, and you weren't necessarily stuck with the hair color you'd been born with. Eventually, I figured that my best bet was outsourcing. If I couldn't do a perfect smoky eye, or get my hair to behave, or find a dress or a shirt that fit and flattered, I could pay people to do it for me.

I was doing okay. And then I had daughters.

My eldest is her grandmother's granddaughter. Lucy dresses, her dad and I joke, like an inmate in a 1980s prison/aerobics video. All pants must be black, gray, or navy blue, with an elastic waist and no tags. Shirts must be cotton, similarly tag-free, in shades ranging from gray to black, although sometimes she'll go crazy and wear purple. Getting Lucy to take her gorgeous honey-blond curls out of her *True Grit*, *Little House on the Prairie* braids and her feet out of her slip-on olive-green Keds and put on a skirt or a dress for High Holidays requires a combination of threats and bribery that would have impressed Torquemada.

Her little sister is . . . well, we're not sure how to explain Phoebe, whose first word was "Mama" and whose first sentence was "Add to cart!" For Phoebe, things can't be frilly or flouncy or sparkly or glittery enough. She lives in dresses, in pink hair bows or headbands, and what she proudly calls her "teenager shoes," a pair of pink-and-red Mary Janes that I bought for Lucy, but could never convince her to wear. She cares about her look . . . and, alas, mine, too. "Mommy, you look pretty," she'll say, when I'm dressed for an event, hair blown straight, clothes chosen by a stylist. Then she'll cock her head, narrow her eyes, and say, "You should wear makeup EVERY DAY." Somewhere, God is laughing. God knows my mother is.

ORBITS

~~~~~~~~~~~~~~~~

RUTH PENNEBAKER

just had a couple of moles taken off my back," our daughter said when we visited her apartment in San Francisco a few years ago. "It's really hard for me to clean off the wound myself—and put the bandage back on. Would you mind doing it, Mom?"

Of course, I wouldn't mind. In fact, I was flattered to be asked. So, I was ready when our twenty-seven-year-old daughter peeled off the bandages and I looked at her back.

But suddenly . . . standing there, swabbing her back with soap, then water, then Vaseline, I was overcome. I don't know whether it happens this way to all mothers, but this is how it happened to me.

You carry a fetus, then a baby, for months. You nourish it with your own, widening body. Then, one day, you give birth. You hold your baby. You nurse her. As the weeks and months pass, you and your husband do everything for her. You feed her, bathe her, diaper her. You control her whole world. In fact, you are her whole world.

Your baby becomes a toddler. Maybe, like us, you have another baby. Years pass . . . and you're pretty sure you and your husband never finish a conversation or even a sentence. Cheerios are permanently stuck to the ceiling, the floors are squishy, and somebody small is always banging a spoon on a high chair or scaling the bookcases like they're a mountain range.

Having a child is like installing a bowling alley in your brain—my husband read that somewhere. I've forgotten who wrote it, but the author is a genius. For years, he was quoted a lot more than Shakespeare around our house.

When we had the time, we recorded our family's height on the back of the pantry door. We were measuring how much they were growing, we told our children, and how much my husband and I were shrinking. When we had the energy, we hired a babysitter and went out for the evening. Sometimes, we were so exhausted, we could hardly wait to come home and fall asleep on the couch with the TV still blaring.

More years passed, and our lives gradually grew calmer. We could take our eyes off our children for a few minutes without being terrified they'd torch the house or impale themselves on salad forks. Our children weren't as wild and we weren't as frantic as we used to be.

Looking back, I realize when our children were young my husband and I revolved around the house where our children were. We always knew where they were, we always knew who they were with. Our schedules were demanding and exhausting, but we had some kind of control.

As they grew older, they came and went more independently. Playing in the neighborhood. Rollerblading. Going to school, to sleepovers. My husband and I were the ones who were fixed and static, and our kids revolved around us in orbits that got bigger and bigger. We were needed, but not as much, not as constantly.

That closed, tight circle of you and your children is outgrown slowly, then with increasing speed as the years pass. Some years, I felt the most important actions my husband and I took were to step back and give our daughter, then her brother, more room. Their worlds expanded far beyond us to college, different cities, other countries.

We were affectionate, but still, we retreated physically. A hug, a kiss, a hand squeeze. That's all. Your child becomes her own person. She doesn't need you hovering over her, touching her, pulling you to her. She needs to leave.

I stood behind my grown daughter, marveling at her strong, beautiful back. The wounds were small, with funny black stitches. It wasn't any blood or gore that overwhelmed me—it was just this kaleidoscope of memories, this primal, fierce wave of love and protectiveness and deep pride. I couldn't bear to feel it too long. I had to step back.

I patched my baby up with clean bandages. Then I sent her back out into the world.

LEAPS AND BOUNDS

~~~~~~~~~~~~~

BARBARA PATRICK

So this is how it went down at the annual carnival in the St. Rose parking lot last summer. My husband and I had a huge public fight because he forced my sweet nine-year-old daughter to ride a scary ride with him by bribing her with cotton candy, which is bad parenting. But that was not as bad as the carnival a decade ago. We (meaning my husband) put my oldest son, when he was three or four, on the swing ride, the one where someone always barfs. He looked way too small for the swing and I had the mother of all panic attacks, sure that he'd fall out. But he didn't. And that torture was one of my greatest life lessons as a mother: that I need to let go sometimes, and when I do they'll be okay, and that the whole thing is one big leap of faith.

But now I stand here humbled by the stupid carnival story. Let me tell you about a real leap of faith. Dropping my three precious children back at school on December 18 in Newtown, Connecticut, was a leap of faith. Yes, that Newtown, where before December 14, packing backpacks and finding missing shin guards was mind-numbing but plenty, and where we still had those twenty-six wonderful souls among us.

I wish there was a grand, universal mothering lesson that I've learned, like, "Top Ten Steps to Survive a Massacre in Your Town" or "Tragedies for Dummies: Tips for Mothering When Evil Visits." But it's not that easy. Of course, I am reminded of the basics—thank God my kids are alive, kiss them more, listen to them. Cherish them. I want to smother them—never remove my lips from their warm, smooth cheeks, and climb into their souls and hang on for dear life. Clichés once grandiose now seem inadequate. It's "unthinkable"—because when I think of what actually happened in the Sandy Hook School, it hurts so badly that I want to, have to stop thinking about it, but I can't. "Seize the day; life is short"—but six-years-old kind of short? Really? It will never make any sense.

Unfortunately, there are logistics to mothering through such a freak show in addition to going through the emotional trauma. First, try to stop crying. Assure loved ones that we're okay, monitor each child's level of grief, check on distraught friends, write sympathy notes, stay abreast of emergency counseling options, try to sleep at night, shelter them from the news on TV, and answer really hard questions like: "Why would someone shoot twenty-six other people? What's a hearse? Are we safe? How would the cops at my school stop another bad man? When will this Sandy Hook 'thing' be over?" And the worst so far, "Do you think they were scared when they died?"

Some days are good—some days we attend basketball games, where our kids are active and happy. We cheer, chat with friends, and yell at the refs. I threw a birthday sleepover party for my daughter, and nine shrieking, hyper girls went to sleep on our den floor with no problem and it felt like a miracle. Some days my kids hang out with the New York Knicks or Mia Hamm at the local sports complex. Most days I try to make good out of bad by fighting for reasonable, safe gun legislation and show my kids how democracy really works. On all days, I try to be a mom who can transport life back to December 13. But that's impossible.

So how to move forward and ensure that their sacred childhoods aren't shattered? I draw inspiration from my kids, who seem strong beyond reason. In my twelve-year-old son's backpack I discovered an essay he'd written about me for school. He wrote, "When I think of my mom, I think of a woman who gives all her effort to her friends and family's happiness. She has positively influenced society by her generosity, her adventurous spirit, and just the smart, intelligent person she is!" Oh my God. I have him duped. He doesn't know that inside, I'm a quivering, terrified mess, begging, pleading to the powers that be, "Please never let it be my child." But that's how he sees me. That's what he needs me to be. And so I'll keep taking that leap of faith called being a mom.

HUMMINGBIRD

A Love Letter to the Mothers at Church

~~~~~~~~~~~~~~~~

LIZ JOYNT SANDBERG

moved here and I had no idea why. In the hindsight of these last two years—you are the ones who crop up everywhere—the most tenacious ones. My guides.

I saw you. Not like "I noticed you"—it was not casual. I mean, I saw you in this room—all the time—all of my watchful energy pulled to your steady balance. I can see your hand on his back—this image is so clear to me. You're sitting about a foot behind him in the pew—he's leaning forward with his armpits pinching the restraint—the pew in front. Your elbow is resting on the pew behind and your hand is in the middle with your fingertips pointing to the right. Your palm is open and touches both of his scapula at once.

I saw you in this room. In all of your ways—all of the very small things you were always humming with. Your bodies moving with perfect economy always in these small tasks that you can't even know now, they're so inseparable from you—the way cells make a body. Your children flowed—flowered right out of these economies. The stream of your care like a fuse and their tiny shocks of hair at the end bursting into the space like fireworks.

I have so many questions for you. Like, "How do you keep humming with all of these moves—all of the pickups of dropped things, finding of lost things, wiping, spooning, holding, whipping of hair—so quick! Into a neat little elastic, pulling up, tucking in, unwrapping, *endless*—how do you keep humming like this and still clearly sing your song?"

"How did you trust the long line of that fuse—your care?" Because that fire—it smolders on the line, taking forever to make that burst of color—that firework. Work. So very much work. Which sometimes—best ones—feels like steady, and consistent and purposeful and love, and fullest fullness, but other times feels like monotony, and numbness and an endless ebbing away.

I have watched you looking exhausted in a million different ways—have cataloged the differences between your tiredness that comes from stress, or sickness, or sleeplessness, or loneliness. But still there is a hum and that smoldering work burning along that fuse. Braiding, and lighting and stoking in this sort of wild and unimaginable sustenance I see you masterful—strong and flexible.

The hum is steady and just right. And in the same way that I now notice the telltale swaying of whose hips have held somebody, your hum is part of this wider secret thing. I saw it and it consumed me—first taking root in my mind before I knew what pulled me, and later a knot in my guts—Ida—my initiation. My amazing membership.

These doings, your being—the sum-hum of these million things was, is, the holiest thing to me. I still feel compelled, whenever we are together to say that I'm just so glad I get to be here looking at you. Every time, with brand-new excitement and discovery, I want to tell you that you are amazing and that I knew from the moment I saw you doing this incredible work that your story was a big deal to me—that I loved you all of a sudden. I know now that I came to be here, to you, on purpose—that your lives were, in part, for me to witness, and that the force of your love for your children drew me from Michigan to Chicago—pulling me with those thousand tiny, unknowable things.

And if I were being perfectly honest—which you really should in a love letter—I would raise my hand every Sunday. It would be a joy and a concern and one of those ripe-fruit-bursting-out-of-its-skin kind of things. And I'd say the same thing over and over because it is always on my mind. "I am so grateful for you. I am so glad for the way that you share your children with us here." And if I were being perfectly honest, I would get crazy and be crying and shaking my head and trying to find bigger and bigger gestures to express just how intense this gratitude feels and I'd try and press my gratefulness into you—my hand still warm from my daughter's back like you taught me—so you'd know, and feel as loved and thoroughly seen as you are.

I'm telling you this so that maybe you can think about yourself this way—who you are to me—when you feel invisible or when you feel like someone's grubby little hands are extracting the last of your wits or will, or when any encouraging thing just feels like a platitude. When you make a steely decision to laugh and play. When you deeply, not as a punch line, want to eat candy in the bathroom with the door closed—when the luxury of that is real and not at all sad.

So all of this is to say that I love you ferociously, and that to me, there is no ebbing away of you but only flourishing. And that even though there are times when it feels like the end of everything, there are other times, like right now, when it feels like a holy gift to flex in these thousand moves and know that I'm humming too—to know that I'm part of this most amazing collection of women doing this most mysterious work. I am so very glad that we are mothers here, together, right now.

Like all the best love letters, this one will just go hoarse and lose its voice. I am trying so hard. It matters so much to me that you know.

A hummingbird. A frantic pulsing performed so expertly that it looks like stillness—like nothing. Moving your whole being all the time until those movements disappear from view. But me? I see you all the time. And I will always hold on to you and count myself blessed, ears tuned to your impossible hum.

ACKNOWLEDGMENTS

While I conceived of and founded the first Listen to Your Mother show, the project's expansion, momentum, and success—along with this book—rest on the shoulders of many.

Thank you to Elisa Camahort Page, along with Jory Des Jardin and Lisa Stone, cofounders of BlogHer, Inc., whose 2009 annual conference made real-life friends out of my Internet friends. *BlogHer's* Community Keynote featured bloggers reading aloud at a podium, and set my producer wheels turning. Thank you for becoming LTYM's first national sponsor, and for continuing to support us as national media sponsor since our 2011 national expansion.

Thank you to Darcy Dederich, longtime friend, coproducer, and stage manager extraordinaire. I'm so grateful that motherhood reunited us as friends, and that LTYM reunited us with The Theater. Thank you to Steve Sperling and the Barrymore Theatre for making that original 2010 show possible, providing us a venue based on zero budget and a big idea, and for serving as LTYM's Mother's Day home in Madison. My fondest gratitude goes to the original cast who brought my LTYM vision to life, and inspired a nation of mother stories: Kaye Becker, Erin Clune, Maggie Ginsberg, Theresa Kim, Dana Maya, Shawnee Parens, Amy Recob, Oroki Rice, Lael Sheber, Erin Ruzicka Trondson, and especially Becky Sewell for years of volunteering and coproducing.

Comedian Suzy Soro, thank you for helping me find my director/producer cojones.

To the incomparable Deb Rox—business strategist, mentor, and beloved friend. Your generosity and patience know no bounds. LTYM would likely be an exquisite and exclusively Madison, Wisconsin, tradition were it not for you. To national team members Taya Dunn Johnson, Stephanie Precourt, and Melisa Wells, your limitless energy, enthusiasm, and expertise have fundamentally shaped LTYM's ability to continue growing and adapting. You three keep me sane, laughing, learning, and prevent me from mucking things up (much). Thank you for your talent, time, and friendship. Sarah Fite, web master and graphics wizard, thank you for your gorgeous logo and design work that not only captures the heart and soul of the project for listentoyourmother-show.com, but gives the show an iconic look.

Of course, LTYM couldn't exist as a national project without our local directors and producers—over one hundred to date. I lack sufficient words of thanks for these visionaries and their behind-the-scenes volunteer/support teams for their hours, heart, and talent. Special thanks to friends Wendi Aarons (with Jennifer Sutton), Stacey Conner (with Elise Raimi), Stephanie Precourt, and Lisa Rae Page Rosenberg (with Leane Vandeman), who first approached me about bringing LTYM home to their towns, and made LTYM a national movement alongside me in 2011. Thank you to Andrea Fellman and Leane Vandeman of Creative Alliance, early champions of LTYM's mission who invited me to bring live-reading events to their gatherings for creative entrepreneurial women. To the thousands of people who've submitted their writing, auditioned, and/or performed with LTYM over the years, thank you for lavishing LTYM with your words, and trusting us with your stories.

Thank you to the corporate sponsors who've kept LTYM afloat, and the dozens of local nonprofit causes we've partnered with across the country, raising over $50,000 as of this writing, in support of women and children in need.

Thank you to my personal cheering section and pit crew: my beloved males—my husband, Ben Imig, and my sons, Elliott and Maxwell; my complicated, large, and loving family; my in-laws; my girlfriends/ saviors; my Novellas and PoP writing groups; and LTYM interns Isabel Dunkerley, Danielle Joyce, and Kendall Ross. Thank you to my first Internet friend and *BlogHer* conference wife, Amy Windsor.

Enormous thanks to my agent, Elizabeth Kaplan, whose vision in that first "I think I see a book here" e-mail, in collaboration with Amy Einhorn and Liz Stein of Putnam/Penguin Random House, resulted in this anthology. Your guidance and expertise helped me to shape a book that captures the heart and spirit of this project. Elizabeth and Liz, thank you for companioning me through this process, listening to my instincts, responding to my hundreds of e-mails and questions with patience, and letting me know what worked, where, and why. Due to the efforts of all of you, LTYM now has a collection of stories we can hold in our hands, and not just in our hearts.

Finally, thank you to all of our audience members at our live shows, on the Internet, and readers of this book for bearing witness to our stories.

ABOUT LISTEN TO YOUR MOTHER, LLC

Founded by humorist Ann Imig in 2010, Listen to Your Mother (LTYM) is a national live-reading series, a grassroots mother-writing movement born of creative online women, and a social media phenomenon garnering millions of impressions. LTYM goes beyond entertainment and performance, creating change through giving voice to stories that might not otherwise be heard, by expanding perspectives on the motherhood experience, and by supporting motherhood through raising awareness and funds for local nonprofit organizations. LTYM has raised over $50,000 to date for causes supporting mothers and families in need.

Locally, LTYM features writers reading their own words about mothering—being a mom, not being a mom, having a mom, not having a mom, losing a mom, finding a mom, and everything in between—live on community stages in celebration of Mother's Day, all over the country in thirty-five cities and counting. LTYM then broadcasts stories globally through our LTYMShow YouTube channel featuring more than 1,000 videos from our past seasons.

Thanks to funding through both corporate and hyper-local sponsorship, and the tireless work of dozens of bloggers-turned-local-directors and -producers, LTYM offers an annual Mother's Day tradition in many cities, while expanding into new towns and metropolises.

In 2015, Listen to Your Mother celebrates its sixth season with the publication of this anthology by G. P. Putnam's Sons.

Learn more at listentoyourmothershow.com

Twitter @LTYMShow

Facebook LISTEN TO YOUR MOTHER

Instagram.com/LTYMShow

Pinterest.com/LTYMShow

YouTube.com/LTYMShow

Wendi Aarons earned a degree in film from the University of Oregon, and immediately went to work in the movie business and the advertising business, where she was yelled at by angry, short men. She then became a stay-at-home mom, where she was yelled at by angry, short men. Her humor pieces have been seen in many, many places, including *McSweeney's*, *Us Weekly's* "Fashion Police," *The Huffington Post*, and *The Wall Street Journal*. In 2007, her letter to Always maxi-pads went viral; then in 2012 she cocreated the widely popular Twitter parody @PaulRyanGosling that also went viral. In addition to writing her blogs, WendiAarons.com (named "Editors' Choice Funniest Blog" by *Parents* magazine) and *The Mouthy Housewives*, Wendi has been an invited speaker at the Texas Conference for Women, *BlogHer*, *Mom 2.0*, and *MomCom*. She is also the founder and three-time coproducer/director of LTYM Austin, and lives in the Lone Star state with her husband, Chris, and sons, Sam and Jack.

Lisa Allen started her first blog, *Back to Allen*, in 2007. A single mom who grew up vowing she'd never have kids, she is slowly (and begrudgingly) coming to grips with the fact that her babies aren't babies anymore. She is a freelance writer, Girl Scout troop leader, volunteer, and stress baker. She prefers red over white and desperately wants to go back to yoga class.

Rebecca Anderson-Brown lives happily in Madison, Wisconsin, with her very handy husband, three busy sons, and two cute but useless dogs. She teaches four-year-old kindergarteners at a Madison nursery school and falls in love with her job again every day. She's also a writer who's currently working on her fourth novel. Writing and reading "Mothering Through the Storm" in LTYM Madison in 2012 was a cathartic moment for her, as she's made it her mission to humanize mental illness by speaking out. It was an emotional experience, but the outpouring of support and thanks she received made it worth every tear. When she isn't busy mothering, teaching, or writing, she splits her time between serial "do-it-yourself-ing," speed-reading, and pretending to understand Minecraft. Rebecca blogs sporadically at amomamongmen.wordpress.com.

Patty Chang Anker is the author of the memoir *Some Nerve: Lessons Learned While Becoming Brave*, a *Parents* magazine "Mom Must-Read" and Books for a Better Life Award finalist that Oprah.com calls "downright inspiring." Named a *Good Housekeeping* "Blogger We Love" and a Circle of Moms "Top 25 Funny Mom" for her blog *Facing Forty Upside Down*, Patty's writing has appeared in numerous publications, including *O, the Oprah Magazine*, WSJ.com, and NPR.org, and she blogs regularly for PsychologyToday.com's "Anxiety" section. A former director of media relations for *The New York Times* and veteran book publicist, Patty is also a certified yoga teacher and a sought-after workshop leader. When she's not writing or teaching she can be found chasing her two daughters across Westchester County, New York. After spending five years facing her fears and helping others face theirs, Patty no longer has a fear of biking, public speaking, or her Chinese parents. But she's still afraid of clowns.

Jennifer Ball is a mother, a writer, and a dog person who lives in Minneapolis. Her award-winning essays about divorce, parenting, and her inappropriate crush on Louis C.K. have appeared on numerous popular websites, and of course on her blog, *The Happy Hausfrau*. Being a part of Listen to Your Mother was a life-changing experience and one she will cherish, always.

Ann Breidenbach is thrilled to bring the birth-mother story to *Listen to Your Mother*. Her memoir-in-progress, *I Love You, Is That Okay?* is the story of motherhood lost and motherhood found. Ann earned her master of fine arts from the Solstice MFA in Creative Writing Program of Pine Manor College, in Boston. Along with writing about motherhood and adoption, Ann blogs about life after fifty. She resides in Columbia, Missouri, with her indomitable miniature Australian shepherd, Tommy.

Stacey Conner loves chai tea lattes and being at home with her children. She hates the cold, finger paints, and Play-Doh. She is a *BlogHer* Voice of the Year for 2010, 2011, 2012, and 2013, and she writes regularly for the online parenting magazine *Mamalode*. Stacey coproduces and directs the Spokane production of Listen to Your Mother. LTYM is one of the true joys in her life and she is inspired every year by the power of storytelling to connect people. She writes about the other joys in her life—four children, adoption, and foster parenting—at anymom myoutthere.com.

Haddayr Copley-Woods is a freelance writer and disabled mother of two living in Minneapolis. You can find her fiction and essays at haddayr.com.

Kathy Curto lives in the Hudson Valley with her husband and their four children. She drives a car with a New York license plate and a Jersey Girl bumper sticker. For a glimpse at her work, please visit www.kathy curto.com.

Jenny Fiore lives in Madison, Wisconsin, with her husband, two children, four hens, and a twenty-two-pound tomcat, dividing her creative time between agency work, magazine writing, and personal writing projects. During her husband's deployment, she volunteered at a local hospice, writing the life stories of people nearing the ends of their lives. She was a 2007 Pushcart Prize Special Mention honoree for creative nonfiction and is the author of the essay collection *After Birth: Unconventional Writings from the Mommylands* (Possibilities Publishing, March 2013).

Jenny Forrester has won several writing awards, including the 2011 Richard Hugo House New Works Competition. Her writing has appeared in *Penduline, Small Doggies Press, Hip Mama, Nailed* magazine, *Indiana Review,* and elsewhere, and she has read onstage with Scott McClanahan and Patrick DeWitt. She coedited *The People's Apocalypse* with Ariel Gore, by Lit Star Press. She curates Portland's Unchaste Readers Series.

Greta Funk is a wife and mom of four and shares her stories on her blog, Gfunkified.com. She has a master's degree she's never used, life experiences she never asked for, and an appreciation for the swiftness with which everything can be taken away. But she also has a sense of humor, and some days, that's all that keeps her sane.

Michelle Cruz Gonzales, the former drummer/lyricist of the female punk band Spitboy, wrote *Pretty Bold for a Mexican Girl: Growing Up Chicana in a Hick Town,* and published "Ana Maria" in *Book Lovers: Sexy Stories from Under the Covers,* by Seal Press. She teaches English and creative writing at Las Positas College, lives with her family in Oakland, California, and blogs at pretty-bold-mexican-girl.com.

Lea Grover is a writer and toddler wrangler living on Chicago's South Side. When she isn't cultivating an impressive dust bunny collection, she waxes philosophic about raising interfaith children, marriage after a terminal cancer diagnosis, and vegetarian cooking on her blog, *Becoming SuperMommy.* When she isn't writing, she can be found singing opera to her children or smeared to the elbow in Townsend pastels.

Natalie Cheung Hall is a native of North Carolina and a rabid UNC–Chapel Hill fan. She now resides in Indianapolis, works as a statistician, and enjoys running, swimming, CrossFitting, cooking, and eating the food she cooks because of the running, swimming, and CrossFitting. She also makes a disproportionately big deal out of simple home projects stemming from her desperate desire to be crafty, like her mother. One home project that is legitimately a big whoop is being a mother to her son, whose four-year-old soul redefines purity and joy each day, and whose giggle fills her daydreams.

Ann Imig, Listen to Your Mother founder and national director, is an award-winning humorist and speaker whose writing has appeared on numerous websites, including *McSweeney's* and *College Humor.* Ann's blog was recognized in *Babble*'s "Top 100 Mom Blogs 2012," and she was named their funniest "Top Twitter Mom" in 2011. *BlogHer* recognized Ann as one of twelve Voice of the Year winners in 2013. *SheKnows* called her one of their "Top 5 Funniest Mom Blogs," and her children call her "The Most Annoying Boss of Everything." Ann lives with her family in Madison, Wisconsin. Find out more at annimig.com.

Taya Dunn Johnson calls herself a native New Yorker, since she was born and raised there; however, the Baltimore metro area has been home since 2012. She has been writing as MrsTDJ since 2006. "Write. Release. Breathe. Repeat" is beyond a tagline for her blog—it's a mantra Taya has adopted and shared with her readers. She's a rebel who breaks blogger rule number one—post on a regular schedule. Her readers don't mind, as they ride the emotional waves while she navigates life as an expressive, vulnerable, humorous, and audacious widowed mother of an autistic toddler. She was introduced to LTYM when she was chosen as a cast member for the 2013 Washington, D.C., show. Taya is a speaker and panelist, most recently at the 2013 Femworking Conference in D.C. In 2014, Taya Dunn Johnson served as coproducer and codirector of the LTYM Baltimore show.

Eddy Jordan is currently an undergraduate at the University of Colorado at Boulder studying theater performance and creative writing. He hopes to continue to pursue theatrical performance in the years to come, a passion instilled in him by his mother. His heart is in comedy, and he can be seen frequenting the Boulder stand-up scene, in sketch comedy shows, and in theater productions at the university. This is his first publication and he is honored to share his mom alongside so many other great mothers.

Nancy Davis Kho is a writer in Oakland, California, whose work appears regularly in *The San Francisco Chronicle* and *EContent* magazine. She's contributed to five anthologies and is finalizing her coming-of-middle-age memoir. An avid music fan, she blogs about the years between being hip and breaking one at MidlifeMixtape.com.

Brian Lavendel is a son, brother, husband, and father. He has grown to appreciate the women in his life and everywhere. He's thankful for the opportunity to express his pride and love for his mother. And at the same time, he feels that every woman has led a heroic life. Now in his ninth career change, he works for social justice, manages apartment buildings, and strives to build community everywhere—often in the midst of cooking, laundry, and dishes.

Jenny Lawson's first book, *Let's Pretend This Never Happened: A Mostly True Memoir*, is an award-winning number one *New York Times* bestseller. Her irreverent humor blog (thebloggess.com) is extremely popular with intellectual misfits. She's been featured on *Gawker*, Salon .com, *Mashable*, *Forbes*, *The Washington Post*, *People*, *O, the Oprah Magazine*, CNN, *Time* magazine, and the *Today* show, and she has fooled many people into thinking she's very important.

Jenifer Joy Madden, a proud mom of three creative, capable grown-up children, is an award-winning community leader, digital communications professor, and multimedia journalist whose work has appeared on ABC News, PBS, Discovery Health Channel, and in *The Washington Post*.

A self-proclaimed "cheerleader for humanity," Jenifer is the force behind the Durable Human book series and website, devoted to helping people realize the amazing powers they have that their smart devices don't.

Jerry Mahoney is a dad, blogger, comedy writer, and the author of the memoir *Mommy Man: How I Went from Mild-Mannered Geek to Gay Superdad*, which tells the whole messy, hilarious, wonderful origin story of his unique family. *Publishers Weekly* called it "uproarious" and "touching," which is pretty much what Jerry was going for. He blogs about life as a gay dad at jerry-mahoney.com. His work has also appeared in *The New York Times, NY Metro Parents, Westchester* magazine, *Scary Mommy*, and the Good Men Project. He regrets that his story requires him to talk about his sperm, and he promises never to raise the topic in person. Jerry lives in New Rochelle, New York, with his husband and two kids.

M. Penny Manson has been blessed with an abundance of material while providing care for her ninety-three-year-old mother and husband with Parkinson's disease. Her poems have been published in the *Zica Anthology, Speak, Write, Dream*, and in *More of Life's Spices, Seasoned Sistahs Still Keepin' It Real*, from Nubian Images Publishing. When she isn't playing on Facebook she is working on a mystery novel series about the "Invisible People."

Jennifer Newcomb Marine is the coauthor of *No One's the Bitch: A Ten-Step Plan for Mothers and Stepmothers* (GPP Life, 2009), with Carol Marine, the stepmom to her two daughters; and *Skirts at War: Beyond Divorced Mom/Stepmom Conflict* (Nest Press, 2013), with Jenna Korf. She's currently at work on *A Light in the Basement: Seven Steps for Transforming Self-Sabotaging Subconscious Beliefs*. She's been featured in *The Washington Post, Publishers Weekly, Psychology Today, The Huffington Post*, and *StepMom Magazine*, and on the *Dr. Phil* show and DivorcedMoms .com. For more, see www.noonesthebitch.com.

Marinka lives in New York City with her two kids, two cats, and a TV set. She's the author of the humor blog *Marinka NYC*, and her writing has appeared in numerous publications, including *The Huffington Post*, *McSweeney's*, BlogHer.com, *Babble*, and her diary. Together with her *Mouthy Housewives* writing partners, Marinka created the popular @ PaulRyanGosling Twitter meme. She has been selected *BlogHer's* Voice of the Year, and has been named one of the best humor bloggers (and human beings) by *Babble* in 2013. She is currently working on her memoir about immigrating to America, titled *From Russia with Baggage*.

Dana Maya is from Colorado and Veracruz, Mexico. She has lived for the last twelve years on the isthmus of Madison, Wisconsin, where she writes professionally, versifies on demand at the Spontaneous Writing Booth, and is at work on a memoir-in-poems about her Mexican-American family. She became irremediably multiplied through the lives of Clio Reyna and Palma Gloria, her daughters. Her mother is Gloria Carmen; her grandmother is Antonia Chiunti Abrego.

Edward McCann is a professional writer whose features and essays have been published in national magazines and literary journals (*American Baby, Better Homes and Gardens, Country Living, Gardener, Good Housekeeping, Ladies' Home Journal, The Sun*, and more). An award-winning television writer/producer and longtime contributing editor at *Country Living*, Ed also writes a blog, *My Rescue Mutt*, which chronicles his adventures with Willie, an eleven-pounder from central Louisiana. Ed is the founder and editor of *Writers Read*, a spoken word showcase for both established and emerging writers, and he's recently completed a memoir titled *Finding George*. He lives and writes in New York's Hudson River Valley.

Angie Miller, a middle and high school librarian in Meredith, New Hampshire, is the 2011 New Hampshire Teacher of the Year and a TED speaker whose writing has been featured in *The Washington Post's*

Answer Sheet, Education Week, The Nerdy Book Club, The Huffington Post, and in the book *American Teachers: Heroes in the Classroom.* She also writes for her two blogs: *Boundless* and *The Contrarian Librarian.* When not being an education nerd, Angie travels, gardens, hikes, and runs a small farm with her patient husband, where they are raising three nearly perfect children, a herd of loving goats, some friendly chickens, a needy dog, and two overly affectionate cats.

Yoon Park emigrated from Seoul, South Korea, at the age of three with her family. Learning to appreciate the transitions and translations between seemingly disparate worlds, she navigates being Korean and American, a high school English teacher and a member of a post-punk band, and a germophobe and a mom. Her almost compulsive need to document the everyday stems from what can best be described as intense nostalgia for what she experiences in the now. Yoon lives in Denver, Colorado, with her curmudgeonly husband and hilarious son.

Barbara Patrick, passionate owner of Bitty Birdie Design, is a quilter and fabric artist who lovingly turns vibrant fabrics into keepsakes of many types. She is also a wife and mother to three fabulous children and is jazzed by travel, being with friends, drinking green tea, and consuming an endless supply of sugar, as well as sewing, reading, and writing.

Mary Jo Pehl is the author of the book *Employee of the Month and Other Big Deals* and has contributed to *Minnesota Monthly,* NPR, *Austin Monthly,* and Salon.com. She is a former writer and actor on the cult television show *Mystery Science Theater 3000.*

Ruth Pennebaker's most recent novel is *Women on the Verge of a Nervous Breakthrough,* which is about three generations of women. Her work has appeared in *The New York Times* and *Texas Monthly.* She blogs at Geezersisters.com.

Sheila Quirke worked as a clinical social worker for ten years before her child was diagnosed with cancer. After her daughter's death, she switched gears and is now a freelance writer, blogs under the name Mary Tyler Mom, and runs a small nonprofit called Donna's Good Things in her sweet little hometown of Chicago. She and her husband are busy raising two growing boys and choosing hope every day.

Robyn Rasberry lives with her family in Fort Worth, Texas, where she is co-owner and managing editor of Robyn Lane Books. She loves her daughter more than the cosmos.

Helen Reese has been a social worker at the Philadelphia Ronald McDonald House since 1998. A former publicist and public relations director, Helen recently completed her first novel, *Project Ex*, which was inspired by her own experiences as a single mother returning to the dating scene following her divorce. She's found happiness, but definitely not normalcy or predictability, in her second marriage to a free-spirited photographer. Between them, they have two sons, two daughters-in-law, two daughters, and three grandchildren.

Vikki Reich writes about the intersection of contemporary lesbian life and parenthood at her personal blog *Up Popped a Fox* and publishes *VillageQ*, a site that gives voice to the experience of LGBTQ parents. She is the codirector and coproducer of Listen to Your Mother Twin Cities and was a 2013 recipient of the Beyond the Pure Fellowship for writers. She lives in Minneapolis with her partner and two kids, who provide the sound track of her life, which involves more beatboxing and improvised pop songs than she ever could have imagined.

Alexandra Rosas is a Mainstage storyteller with nationally acclaimed The Moth. She writes culture and memoir for various online websites and is a contributor to several anthologies. You can follow her on her personal blog, *Good Day, Regular People*.

Lisa Page Rosenberg is a former writer/producer for television. She is a current class chaperone/soccer mom for PTA. She has been chosen by *BlogHer* as a Voice of the Year and her daily family humor blog, *Smacksy*, has been included in "best of" lists from *Parade* magazine and She .Knows.com. She lives in Southern California with Mr. Rosenberg and their son, Bob.

Jen Rubin is a former New Yorker living in Madison, Wisconsin. An obsessive maker of mixtapes and the best challah baker in town, she has worked for social change throughout her career. Jen has told stories at the Milwaukee Moth story slam, Milwaukee Moth grand slam, and Moth Mainstage at the Brooklyn Academy of Music. Currently Jen is writing a memoir about Radio Clinic, the appliance store her family has owned since 1934 on the Upper West Side of Manhattan.

Liz Joynt Sandberg is a Chicago-based writer and performer. Currently, she can be seen with Infinite Sundaes at Second City, with Lola at iO Chicago, and with Storytown Improv—a fully improvised musical for kids and their grown-ups! She occasionally writes online for websites like *Second City Network* and *The Huffington Post*.

Robert Shaffron and his husband, John, are permitted to remain in their residence through the generosity of their two magnificent sons, Benjamin and Jordan, in Maplewood, New Jersey. Robert has been, variously, a playwright, an advertising creative director, stock boy, dishwasher, actor/waiter, and is currently a stay-at-home LGBT activist. He also bakes a wicked lemon square.

Margaret Smith started her comedy career in Chicago, where she studied at the Second City Theater. She is well-known for her stand-up comedy, and her credits are many, including six Emmy Awards for writing and producing on the *Ellen DeGeneres Show*. She recently moved to

Austin, Texas, with her children, where she spends her time trying to figure out why she moved to Austin, Texas.

Mery Smith is a mother, a wife, a daughter, and friend. She lives in the Pacific Northwest and would only trade mountains for ocean. She loves to dance and sing with her children especially. She believes that kindness is a revolution—wherever you are is a good place to begin. You can read more about her babies, her chickens, and her truth at merysunshine.com.

Meggan Sommerville has been writing nearly her whole life as an outlet for her creative energy. She finally found a public outlet to share her Christian faith, her life as a transgender woman, and her experiences being a mom on her blog *Trans Girl at the Cross*.

Megan Stielstra is the author of the essay collection *Once I Was Cool* (Curbside Splendor, 2014). Her work is included in *The Best American Essays 2013, Poets & Writers Magazine, The Rumpus,* and elsewhere. She teaches creative writing at Columbia College Chicago and is the literary director of the 2nd Story storytelling series.

Jennifer Sutton is the mother to children, cats, one very old dog, and, at any given time, at least a few hamsters. She is also a recovering lawyer and the social media hostess for Purina Cat Chow. Jennifer recently bid adieu to being a single mom of three and married again, to her great surprise and delight. She lives with her husband, Armando, and their collective four kids in Austin, Texas. Her days are full of all varieties of laughter, tears, tedium, and triumph. Through it all, one constant remains: she writes it down.

Tasneem Grace Tewogbola is a writer whose roots run from West Africa to upstate New York. While her different titles mother/wife/daughter/ sister/sistafriend/seamstress/runner/reader/gardener/editor/sojourner point to other skills and interests, it is ultimately her love of stories, cultural connection, and storytelling that inspires nearly every dimension of her life. She and her husband, Zuberi, raise five daughters in Nashville, Tennessee.

Kate St. Vincent Vogl teaches at The Loft Literary Center in Minneapolis. National ABC news featured her book, *Lost and Found: A Memoir of Mothers*. She writes both fiction and nonfiction. Her latest work appears in *Bellingham Review*. Vogl graduated cum laude from Cornell University and from the University of Michigan Law School.

Zach Wahls is a sixth-generation Iowan, an advocate for LGBTQ rights, an Eagle Scout, and the cofounder of Scouts for Equality, the national campaign to end discrimination in the Boy Scouts of America. His testimony about his two-mom family before the Iowa House Judiciary Committee was YouTube's most watched political video of 2011. He is a Truman Scholar and the author of the national bestseller *My Two Moms: Lessons of Love, Strength, and What Makes a Family*.

Nadine C. Warner has worked as a lawyer, IT consultant, admissions director, TV producer, and finally (!) creative director for The Bricolage Group, a corporate communications company she founded with her partner. When she's not playing air traffic controller to her three spirited kids and übertolerant dog, she writes about her completely ordinary life at nadinecwarner.com.

Jennifer Weiner is the number one *New York Times* bestselling author of ten novels, including *Good in Bed*, *In Her Shoes*, and *All Fall Down*. She lives with her family in Philadelphia.

Stefanie Wilder-Taylor is the author of five books, including *Sippy Cups Are Not for Chardonnay* and her latest, *Gummy Bears Should Not Be Organic*. On TV she hosts the late-night show *Parental Discretion with Stefanie*

Wilder-Taylor on NickMom. She also cohosts the hit podcast *For Crying Out Loud*. She lives in Los Angeles with her husband and three sporadically charming daughters. Although she's sober, she may have a serious problem with sugar-free Popsicles.

Amy Wilson is the author of *When Did I Get Like This?* (Harper Collins, 2010) and the play *Mother Load*, which toured to sixteen cities nationwide after its hit run off-Broadway. As an actor, Amy also costarred in *The Last Night of Ballyhoo* on Broadway, appeared as a series regular on two sitcoms (NBC's *Daddio* and ABC's *Norm*), and has guest-starred in many other TV shows and films. She has written for magazines like *Redbook* and *Parenting*, and websites like CNN, NPR, and *The New York Times*. Blog: whendidigetlikethis.com.

Katie Wise, professional birth junkie, is a doula, childbirth educator, pre- and postnatal yoga teacher, birth advocate, and the owner and founder of Yo Mama Yoga and Family Centers. Her work and writing have been featured in *Whole Life Times*, *Yogi Times*, *Los Angeles Daily News*, *Special Delivery*, *The Sun* magazine, the upcoming *Home Birth Handbook*, and NPR. She is the host of the Mother's Advocate *Healthy Birth Your Way: Six Steps to a Safer Birth* video series. Katie is proud mama of a boy and girl. Find more about Katie at yomamayoga.com and yomamablog.com.

Ann Stewart Zachwieja lives in Boulder, Colorado, with her family, dogs, and horse, enjoying the beauty, people, and activities of the area. Having moved to Boulder after many years in Seattle, Ann visits the Pacific Northwest as often as possible to spend time with lifelong friends and balance out what can't be found in Colorado—the large bodies of water, the marine activities, and the Asian influences so prevalent in the Northwest. Ann loves to travel and looks forward to taking her daughter back to China someday to meet her Aunties and absorb where she started her life.